Letters Home

Letters Home

◆

Musings of an American Expatriate Living in Japan

Todd Jay Leonard

iUniverse, Inc.
New York Lincoln Shanghai

Letters Home
Musings of an American Expatriate Living in Japan

iUniverse, Inc.

For information address:
iUniverse, Inc.
2021 Pine Lake Road, Suite 100
Lincoln, NE 68512
www.iuniverse.com

ISBN: 0-595-28309-8 (pbk)
ISBN: 0-595-74843-0 (cloth)

Printed in the United States of America

To Shingo Ono

Contents

Acknowledgments

This book had its genesis in a newspaper column I wrote for *The Shelbyville News*, Shelbyville, Indiana. The content of these articles largely dealt with the everyday-life experiences I encountered regularly while living and working in Japan. At the suggestion of more than several regular readers of this column, I set out to rewrite and edit some of the more interesting essays. The end result is this book.

It is with great pleasure that I publicly thank *The Shelbyville News* for giving me a weekly column. This year-long series allowed me to put down onto paper my experiences of living and working in Japan over the past fifteen years, while at the same time offering the general community a glimpse into a foreign culture and a slice of my life in Japan.

Living half-way around the world, I depended upon a number of people for weekly feedback. I am most appreciative to Brian Culp who edited the published weekly versions; Steve Talbert, a fellow columnist, who initially suggested that I write a column about my life in Japan; Chris Wissing, Cynthia Eiler, and my mother and stepfather, Joann and Jack Brees, who faithfully read each column; and all of the other people who wrote to me each week with comments about the articles' contents. Being a teacher myself, I was thoroughly pleased to learn that a number of teachers in elementary, middle, and high schools around central Indiana regularly used my articles in their weekly lessons.

Conversations with a number of my Japanese friends and colleagues (my "cultural informants") helped me to further develop my ideas and define my thinking while putting this book together. I wish to publicly acknowledge all of those who read parts or all of this manuscript, sparing me from inaccuracies in detail and oversights in assessment. Of course, while they accept no responsibility for any defects, I am confident that their suggestions and candid criticisms have made these essays comparatively better.

To all of these I extend my heartfelt gratitude.

Nota bene: Any prices used in the essays are based on an exchange rate of 120 yen to $1.00 US dollar.

Prologue

The idea for this book actually originated from a weekly column I wrote for my hometown newspaper on Japanese culture and my impressions of Japan. The original series was called "Letters Home: A Hoosier in Japan."

The weekly articles were a huge hit in my hometown and attracted quite a following. Perhaps the reason why it was so popular amongst the readership was because many people were intrigued by Japan but didn't know much about its culture, customs and traditions. The writing style—like personal letters—appealed to many people because each column covered everyday-life situations that I encountered while living in Japan. Readers were able to connect personally with what I had experienced, which made it seem real and authentic to them.

All over the United States, as well as in my hometown of Shelbyville, Indiana, Japanese people are a part of the community; some marry Americans and relocate to the US; others come to work in both Japanese and US owned industry; while still others come to visit and get to know individual Americans through sister-city programs and exchanges.

This interest in things Japanese generated very positive feedback from the townspeople, and at several people's suggestion, I set out to rewrite and edit some of the more interesting articles. The end result is this book, a series of letter-essays relating my impressions and ideas about being an American living in Japan. The content of each consists of information that has been borrowed primarily from my own personal experiences while living in Japan, and from factual information about the various aspects of Japanese culture—differing attitudes, customs, and traditions—as I see and interpret them.

The ideas and impressions contained herein are my own, so I certainly cannot speak for every Westerner living in Japan—nor would I want to because each and every foreigner who calls Japan home would have a different interpretation of and reaction to the same situation; they are mine and mine alone.

As a general point of reference, to compare and contrast cross-cultural differences, I do refer to the United States and my experience of being born and raised in the Midwest throughout my essays. This is in no way meant to disenfranchise other Westerners or to give the impression of being "American-centered." Simply, it is what I am and what I know best; it is a compilation of writings about an American teacher living and working in Japan.

My first introduction to Japan was as an elementary school child when a Japanese art teacher taught classes at my school. I had heard about Japan from TV programs, magazines, and books (there was a huge "Japan-boom" for some years after the Tokyo Olympics took place in 1964). This teacher, though, really intrigued me. She left her home and family—everything that she knew and was dear to her—to come to my little town to teach art. Her accent, mannerisms, and style of dress fascinated me.

This fascination continued throughout my life and as a 17-year-old high school student, I finally had an opportunity to experience Japan first-hand. I spent the summer as a Youth for Understanding (YFU) exchange student living in a suburb of Tokyo.

This experience quite literally changed my life. I had been bitten by the Japan bug and was chronically smitten by its people, culture, tradition and history. That same summer, the son of the family I stayed with came back to the United States with me and lived with my family for a year. By the end of his year in Indiana, my entire family and circle of friends were "Japanophiles."

As a university student I settled for studying Japanese history because in the early 1980's few Japanese language programs existed. I did have an opportunity to return to Japan for a summer as a participant on the 34th Japan-American Student Conference (JASC). This experience served to reinforce my desire to return to Japan for a longer period of time.

In between my two trips to Japan, I lived in Spain and Costa Rica. Each place, although unique and interesting in its own right, never replaced my sincere desire to return to Japan.

In 1989, after finishing a graduate program in history, I was offered a chance to live and work in Hirosaki, Japan as an Assistant Language Teacher (ALT) on the Japan Exchange and Teaching (JET) Program(me). For two and one-half years I taught English alongside a Japanese teacher of English in junior high schools all over the Tsugaru area of Aomori Prefecture, on the main island of Honshu.

It was during this time that I was offered an associate professorship at a local university, where I continue to teach today—Cross-Cultural Understanding, Comparative Culture and Studies, and English—in the Faculty of Liberal Arts.

Little did I know, as I sat in that Japanese art teacher's class as a little boy, that I someday would leave all that I know and love to teach Japanese children in a country and culture far away from my roots and home. My yearning for cross-cultural understanding has turned into a lifetime vocation.

Taking a Bath...Japanese-Style

Several years ago, a good friend from the United States came to visit me in Japan. I wanted her to experience every facet of Japanese culture during her short visit, so I planned our schedule meticulously. I dragged her to countless temples and shrines; we climbed to the top of the castle in my city; we took the bullet and sleeper trains; we went to the top of Tokyo Tower to see the expansiveness of Tokyo; and we sang authentic karaoke in a "snack" (a small establishment that features singing and small snack-like food items, as well as drinks). We did everything.

Probably, though, the most memorable experience for her was going to the public bath. Japan's custom of communal bathing is world-renowned...and a custom that most Americans (along with eating raw horsemeat and grilled eel) are usually more than glad to pass on. This friend, though, was such a good sport and was willing to try anything. So, off we went with our little "bath kits" of towels, soap, shampoo, and Japanese-style washcloths (long and narrow) in hand to experience this very Japanese tradition.

Today, the majority of public baths are segregated, so she was on her own. I gave her a quick lecture on the rules of etiquette for public bathing: 1) leave your towel and all clothes in the change room; 2) find an open spot along the wall with a mirror, bucket and stool; 3) wash thoroughly with soap and water *before* getting into the bath; 4) use the washcloth to partially cover the important areas as you make your way to the bath; 5) slowly ease your way into the bath because it is scalding hot; 6) if in doubt, inconspicuously observe the behavior of others and follow their example.

Hot spring baths, or *onsen*, that have a year-round, outside (*rotenburo*) facility of bathing will often have co-ed bathing. City baths, however, are separated by a wall, with the ceiling area open to both sides. An elderly woman or man usually works at these facilities part-time, sitting high up in a chair that has a view of both sides. Perhaps this is in case anyone needs help, or if someone slips and falls. For whatever reason, it is a bit disconcerting the first time to be so exposed to so many people with no privacy. Japanese people are very polite though, and never gawk (to stare would be rude), so people go about their own business and largely ignore the other people bathing...unless, of course, there is a foreigner present.

After a few minutes, while I was bathing, I heard a raucous on the other side of the partition. I thought, "Uh-oh...what kind of trouble has my friend gotten into?" I yelled over and she assured me everything was OK, and then I heard laughter, which relieved my apprehension.

Later, she explained to me what had happened. Apparently, as she was sitting down on the tiny stool, it slipped out from under her and the stool and bucket went flying across the room, practically knocking an old lady off her stool. The other bathers, all elderly women, were concerned for her, and not being able to tell them in Japanese that she was all right, she resorted to gestures to convey that she was indeed fine. Hence, all of the laughter I heard.

When my mother visited, I took her to an *onsen* also, but we went with a female friend so that she could show my mother what to do. Everything was going fine, or so my friend thought, until an elderly woman called out to her and said, "You had better get that foreign woman out of the bath before she explodes!" My friend looked at my mother and instantly realized that she had stayed in the water too long. My mother was as red as a lobster.

Japanese people get in and out of the water several times during one bath, a point I failed to mention to my mother. So, not knowing, she just stayed in the water. After being extracted from the bath, Mother was fine, albeit a bit dizzy and wobbly around the knees.

Public bathing in hot springs is a very popular outing for families in Japan. Each mineral or sulfur spring has its own curative benefits and people go for a whole host of aches and pains from arthritis to more serious health conditions, and with great success. Hot spring bathing is even used to help couples with fertility issues. A good American friend and her husband had been desperate to have a child and had tried everything to no avail. She was prepared to return to the US to be artificially inseminated at great financial cost. Her Japanese doctor, however, suggested that they go to a small hot spring near where she lived for the weekend and to bathe several times each day. It did the trick; nine months later they had a healthy bouncing baby boy.

Although public bathing in very hot water with complete strangers takes some getting used to, as those who have done it can attest, it is well worth it because it is so very refreshing and relaxing. A trip to Japan should include this very traditional and exhilarating custom for anyone wishing to experience the "real" Japan.

Cherry Blossom Season

Every year, from the first signs of spring until summer is almost upon us, Japan becomes awash in cherry blossoms—light pink, flowering trees that cast a surreal glow upon the urban and rural landscapes. Perhaps the closest event to this that we have in the United States is in Washington, DC where the entire monument area turns "pink" from all of the blooming cherry trees (originally gifts to the US from Japan).

The Japanese become a people obsessed during cherry blossom season. Even the nightly news usually leads with a "cherry blossom update" which follows the buds from when the first blooms peek out in the southern-most island of Japan, until the end of May when the last trees bloom in the northern-most island of Hokkaido. News reporters are sent on location to give detailed reports of the progress of the blossoms and to comment upon the best places to view them. Special weather maps are used to point out the progression of the cherry blossoms. Digitally, these maps gradually turn a pale pink, the color slowly inching its way up the map of the country, signifying where the trees are in full bloom.

The city where I live, Hirosaki, has one of the most spectacular cherry blossom festivals in the country. Every year, for a week, when the blossoms are at their most glorious, hundreds-of-thousands of people make their way here by boat, train, bus and plane to stroll through the medieval castle grounds in order to get a first hand look at the thousands of strategically placed trees dotting the castle area.

What makes our festival all the more special is the castle—Hirosaki boasts the northern-most original castle structure in Japan. Most castles were destroyed during feudal wars by rival shoguns or struck by lightening and burned down. Unlike European castles made of stone, all of Japan's castles were made of wood. Earthquakes and stone buildings do not mix as well as wooden structures do; wood offers more flexibility to withstand the rumbling and tumbling of the frequent tremors and quakes that plague Japan on a regular basis.

Some years, the blossoms bloom early (to the chagrin of all who have had hotel and travel reservations booked for a year). Every year, I do my yearly *hanami*, the custom of sitting under the blooming cherry trees with a group of friends or colleagues. The main form of entertainment during these outings is eating and drinking. People carry in huge tarps to place on the ground for everyone in the group to sit on, as well as spreading out banquet-like amounts of food for all to enjoy, and coolers upon coolers filled with an assortment of spirits like beer, wine, and the favorite among the festival attendees, *sake*. This tradition is enjoyed by old and young alike and can be quite a cross-cultural experience for an outsider like myself.

Most people may not realize this, but Japan is a country that likes to drink…and a lot. The majority of get-togethers, whether they are in someone's home or in a restaurant, are centered on the drinking of alcohol. There is no real social stigma to being drunk and behaving poorly because of alcohol in Japan, unlike in the United States where people are offended because of someone's alcohol induced unruliness and rude behavior.

It is during these times of "nomunication" (a coined word which takes the Japanese word for "drinking" and combines it with the English word "communication") that one gets a glimpse of Japanese people's true colors, outside of the shackles of office protocol and societal obligation. The shyest of people, who never make a spectacle of themselves at work or in public, are much less inhibited after a few drinks (coupled with the naturally intoxicating effect of the cherry blossoms swaying overhead) to get up and belt out a karaoke song or to do a traditional Japanese dance…or to state their true opinions to those around them. It is during these times that Japanese people feel they can be truly open and honest. If their honesty is too candid (i.e. offensive) with a supervisor or a colleague during one of these soirees, then all is forgiven the next morning and blamed upon the alcohol. The incident is rarely, if ever, mentioned again.

Cherry blossom season is my favorite time of the year in Japan because it is such an entrenched part of Japanese culture. The festival itself reminds me more of a July 4th outing in a park rather than a festival. Many of the same components, however, exist in both—food, drink, camaraderie, music, special programs, a parade and most importantly, enjoyment by all.

America…A Smoker's Hell?

Every so often, I have the unique opportunity to travel from Japan to the United States with a group of students from my university so they can participate in a 3-week home-stay and English study program. These short exchange programs offer them a glimpse of American culture and a chance to learn English firsthand. It truly is a great educational opportunity for them, but equally valuable is the cross-cultural education it affords me. It allows me to see the US—not as a native of America who grew up there—but as an outsider, of sorts, through the wide-eyes of students who experience for the very first time different cultural attitudes, language as it is actually spoken, traditions, and customs.

Recently, I chaperoned one such group of university students on an exchange to the US. As usual, their comments and observations amazed me. One student, for instance, innocently related to me how her host family ate ice cream *every* night before bed, "Huge bowls with chocolate sauce and peanuts," she said with a bit of shock in her voice. It was as if she had stumbled upon some deeply hidden cultural secret. The sense of awe and wonderment in her voice was obvious.

Her amazement was for good reason; in Japan, good ice cream tends to be quite pricey (anywhere from $7–$9 a quart) so that means the portions in Japan are generally much smaller than those in the US. A gallon of ice cream in a Japanese freezer is unheard of—not because of the cost as much as a lack of space to store it. A gallon container would simply take up too much room in a Japanese freezer. This student admitted to me that she gained 10 lbs. in three weeks.

Another student had a much more pressing dilemma. He was a smoker, and America is rapidly becoming a smoke-free society. Since I'm a strident non-smoker myself, I guess I never really noticed or thought about how difficult it is to find a public place to smoke in the US.

Japan is currently like America was 25 years ago. The smoking sections in restaurants are small (if any are offered at all) and smoking is permitted in just about every location. In fact, a "non-smoking" table is often situated next to a "smoking" table with no real difference except it doesn't have an ashtray. So, the meaning is lost in Japan; non-smokers don't like being around smoke while eating, hence the desire to be in a smoke-free environment. Having the table next to you puffing away is basically equal to being at a smoking table.

When I asked this student what he found to be the biggest difference between America and Japan, his answer was immediate: "Japan is a smoker's heaven, and America is a smoker's hell." He's right. Smoking in Japan is still very entrenched in all facets of society that there is no social taboo whatsoever about lighting up.

Even the women's movement in Japan, although strides behind that of other Western countries, has for better or for worse, given women the courage to light up in public places. This is something that the mothers and grandmothers of young women today would never have dreamed of doing. Up until just a few years ago, most women who smoked were "closet" smokers, only lighting up at home and never in public because it was considered not to be lady-like.

This has all changed and in a big way. In the decade or so that I have been teaching university students, the percentage of young smokers has steadily been increasing each year, especially among female smokers. Part of the problem is that smoking is portrayed in Japan as being sleek, glamorous and cultured. Added to this is the peer pressure from friends in high school and in university to start the habit. Also, the cost is much cheaper in Japan than in the US. Ironically, tobacco is one of only a few bargains available.

Although the antismoking movement is making some headway in Japan, it has a long way to go before it is at the point the movement is in the US. When I first arrived in Japan "no smoking" signs were regularly ignored in elevators and even in movie theaters. Today, people are more courteous and "smokers' corners" (areas for smokers) are used more widely. Japanese smokers currently respect a "non-smoking" car of a train and respect posted "no smoking" areas...for the most part. In Tokyo, some restaurants are actually beginning to segregate smokers and non-smokers in designated areas. In time, this trend will spread to other parts of Japan.

The greatest lesson my smoking student learned on his trip to America was that patience is a virtue. The 12 hour smoke-free flight, the completely smoke-free airport facilities, and subsequent no smoking policy of his host family made him reflect inwardly on his habit. He briefly quit, but resumed after returning to "smokers' heaven."

Simple Pleasures of a Bygone Era

Attention to detail is a hallmark of Japanese businesses. Take for instance a regular hair salon. Getting one's haircut and having a shave is a very relaxing proposition and something that I always look forward to each month...whether I need or not.

I go to two places regularly, one in my city and the other in Tokyo. The Tokyo shop is pricey ($60.00 for a haircut) but well worth the added cost for all of the pampering I receive. Upon arrival, my coat and bag are securely tucked away in a closet for safe-keeping (generally shops are small and there is not a lot of space to have coats and bags lying about).

Then, I am escorted to a waiting area where the "hair designer" comes to consult with me about the actual haircut. At this point, I am offered a cup of tea or coffee and given magazines. A few minutes later an apprentice "hair designer" comes to fit me in a wrap-around *kimono*—a garment to protect my clothes from shampoo and slivers of hair.

Next, comes the most luxurious shampooing and head massage imaginable. A sheer cotton cloth is gently laid over my face. I have been told that it is in order to protect the customer from flying suds during the shampooing, but after living here for so long, I think it has more to do with the discomfort of the shampooer being so close (face to face) with the customer. It is simply more modest, and even polite, for both parties not to have direct eye contact during such an intimate procedure. After all, Japanese people tend to be shy and avoid direct contact whenever possible. In addition, a heavy towel is laid over my arms and legs which was probably originally adopted for the benefit of women who wear dresses. Being hoisted up in a chair, laying flat on one's back is not always the most flattering position to be in.

The shampoo process is lengthy, with multiple layers of shampooing and conditioning taking place. As the shampooer finishes, s/he does a quick but gentle scalp massage. After placing a scalding hot towel gently under my neck, the hair is thoroughly towel dried. This simple step is the most relaxing and soothing. Hot towels are used widely in Japan—especially at restaurants to allow customers to refresh themselves—a custom that I fully embrace.

After being escorted to the actual chair where the haircut will be performed by the stylist, excuse me, "hair designer," again I am offered something to drink and magazines to flip through. The haircut is slow and methodical. I never get the feeling that the person is in a hurry or is being rushed, even if others are patiently waiting.

Before blow-drying the hair, another person comes to do a full shoulder and upright back massage. Starting at the head, using *shiatsu*-related pressure points, the staff person gradually works down the neck, shoulders and back. This is indeed invigorating, especially for those who must venture back out into the concrete jungle of Tokyo. By this point of the haircut, I feel like a wet-noodle from all of the pummeling and kneading...albeit a relaxed noodle.

After paying, a staff person slips my coat back on me and hands me my bag; another person is at the door ready to open it. I am then escorted to the street by the person who actually cut my hair. Meanwhile, everyone is bowing and thanking me for my patronage. The whole process, from start to finish, takes a full two hours.

Another treat I enjoy, and one which I had never experienced while living in the US, is the old fashioned cut and shave. Growing up, I remember the downtown area of my hometown being dotted with the tell-tale red, white and blue barber poles, but I never had received a cut and shave in one. Today, these are largely a part of history as most people go to stylists rather than barbers. In Japan, though, barbershops with the identical poles are quite plentiful.

Going in for a shave is, again, a relaxing experience. My face is prepared with hot towel, after hot towel, and the barber meticulously shaves me and trims my mustache. Also, a custom here is to have your ears cleaned by barbers, as well as the fine inner hairs trimmed. The first time I had this done, I was admittedly nervous. The long metal instrument being put into my ear went against all advice I had been given growing up: "Never put anything smaller than your elbow in your ear."

This, however, is not the case now as I relish having this procedure done, as well as having my forehead shaved. Yes, in Japan, they take a fine blade and gently scrape the entire face—forehead, tops of the ears, and the bridge of the nose. Places where you never knew hair even grew!

Living in Japan sometimes takes me back to the bygone era of my childhood in that many service-oriented businesses still flourish here—the neighborhood drycleaners, the mom & pop market, the shoe shine corner, and of course the old fashioned barber shop. Simple pleasures.

Living as an "Outsider"

Let's face it…no matter how long I live in Japan, and no matter how fluent my Japanese becomes, I will always be a *gaijin* (literally an "outsider"; a foreigner). On the other hand, an Asian who immigrates to the US, after time, can assimilate into mainstream American society because Asian-Americans are numerous and are but one thread in the beautiful tapestry that makes up American society.

I, however, stand out like a sore thumb in Japan and this will never change…and nor do I really want it to. I *am* American and I am quite proud of my heritage and ethnicity. I just happen to live and work in Japan.

One aspect of being a person who enjoyed being a member of the majority, and who then suddenly found himself thrust into being in a minority, is the perspective I have received from this unique experience. The Japanese are a very group-oriented people and come from a clannish tradition which inherently makes people suspicious of outsiders or non-group members. For me, it has been a tremendous learning experience, both culturally and personally. I have had first-hand experience in knowing what it feels like to be a member of a "minority."

Growing up as a member of the cultural, linguistic, and ethnic "majority" made me somewhat unaware, perhaps, of the feelings others may have had who were in the minority. This life-experience of living in Japan has given me pause for reflection, which in turn has made me much more sensitive to the feelings and attitudes of those in the United States who are members of minority groups.

I am often asked by family and friends on trips back home if I ever experience discrimination in Japan. The answer is a resounding "yes." It may be a different type of discrimination, but it is discrimination nonetheless. Japan, just like every other place in this great, big world—from the smallest tribe to the biggest metropolis—has racism and some discriminatory practices. As humans we tend to concentrate on the few differences between groups of people and gloss over the overwhelming percentage of similarities that we all share. Japan is no different.

Granted, perhaps because of the past 60 years of post World War II influence the United States has had on Japan, I (as a white American male) have much less experience in overt discrimination as, let's say, a Southeast Asian woman of color does. But it exists, albeit subtlety. For instance, often times on a train all of the seats will fill up with the exception of the one next to the "foreigner." Is this racism or just cultural shyness? It is difficult to say for sure, but I had an interesting experience recently on a train which illustrates my point.

I was sitting in a row-seat and the space next to me was empty. The train quickly filled up and in no time the seat next to me and one other, across from me, were the only empty spaces. People were standing all about me, and just as the door was to close, an older, well-dressed, fadingly attractive woman slipped in and headed for the empty seat next to me. As she approached, she realized that I was a *gaijin* and stopped. Instantly, she spotted the other empty seat, and without hesitation, she sat down.

The reason why no one else had taken the seat across from me was because it was next to a homeless man who had rather, well extremely, poor personal hygiene. The woman's facial expression quickly changed from that of self-satisfaction at nabbing a seat on a crowded train to one of pure torture. Her mind was so easy to read: "I should have sat next to the neatly dressed and freshly showered foreigner."

At the next stop, she got up and moved to the seat next to me. As she sat down, I politely shifted to the side to give her more space. She acknowledged this kindness with an appreciative bow of the head, which I returned in kind. She then let out a huge sigh of relief. Again she resumed a very self-satisfied look on her face, perhaps not so much for having finagled yet another coveted seat on a crowded train, but more so because she had overcome a personal phobia—sitting next to a wild-eyed *gaijin*.

Maybe to make up for her earlier reaction, she politely made conversation with me. I was happy to oblige her because it might just make a positive difference in her attitude toward foreigners in the future—we aren't all bad, and actually some of us are even quite pleasant. So the next time she comes face to face with another "outsider" in a similar situation, she may react differently than she had that morning.

One thing I have learned over the past decade or so while living in Japan is that internationalization and general acceptance occurs one person at a time. Actions do speak louder than words.

No Checks... Cash Only, Please

One American convenience that I miss a great deal while living in Japan is using "personal checks" to pay for things in stores. Japan doesn't have the custom of writing checks or being paid by checks. The concept of a "paycheck" that an employee is given weekly or monthly is foreign here. Salaries are often paid in cash, or direct deposited into the person's personal bank account.

I remember very clearly when I got paid the first time, shortly after arriving in Japan—it was quite a culture shock. In the late afternoon, on a Friday, the office lady in charge of payroll came to my desk with an envelope bulging with money. She handed it to me and just walked away. I was speechless. I couldn't believe that I had to carry around an entire month's salary in my bag until Monday! I hid it around my apartment until the banks opened the next week, but it made me very nervous nonetheless. America really is beginning to become a cashless society. Between using checks and credit cards, people don't need a lot of "cash" to do everyday business.

Japan, on the other hand, is very much a cash-based society. Back in those days, the "cash" would arrive earlier than it did that first time, and a bank employee would come to our office and go from desk to desk to take our "deposits." The banker would give us a "receipt of deposit" and go on his/her merry way. In general, Japan is a pretty safe country and it was rare for one of these bank people to be robbed. It's all the more amazing when considering that these people (after collecting an entire office's salaries) would then go out into the street with the equivalent of tens of thousands of dollars in their bags.

Today, I think this custom has largely given way to direct deposit. This system is very convenient because just about everything can be directly deposited into or withdrawn out of one's personal account. I have all of my utilities, telephone, fitness club fee, and taxi service withdrawn automatically from my account. Later, I get a receipt in the mail. It's a nice system because you never have to worry about due dates and getting the bill paid on time to avoid late fees. You do, however, have to make sure that your account has enough money to cover all of your monthly expenses.

Going to the bank in Japan can be a very relaxing experience all in all. Customers do have to wait a bit because the actual transaction one does with the teller has to be handed off—no matter how trivial or how complicated—to a colleague and a superior who then double-check the calculations thoroughly. This custom is largely cultural and has to do with the "group oriented" aspect of Japanese society. In case of a mistake, blame can be divided later on among several employees rather than just one.

To pass the time, banks offer sofa-like seating in long rows to sit on while waiting and an assortment of magazines and newspapers are provided for customers to peruse. When friends visit me, they often need to change US dollars into yen at some point, so I take them to my local bank. They are always very impressed with the full-service treatment they receive.

A greeter is often placed at the door to assist customers initially and to direct them to where they need to go; if a customer needs to do more involved banking (like changing money), the person is offered a seat at a counter and is oftentimes served a hot cup of Japanese green tea to sip while conducting the business at hand. Because the economy has been languishing for the past decade and longer, banks do all they can to attract customers. Service with a smile and a deep bow is guaranteed.

In addition, Japanese banks usually give the customer some type of gift. Gift giving, in general, is an engrained part of Japanese society. It can be anything from a package of tissue or candy to more elaborate gifts like slippers, coin purses and/or small appliances. Every year, in January, I am given umpteen calendars and agendas, as well as small boxes of laundry powder, notebooks and the like as "thank you" gifts for my business. It's a nice custom, I suppose, but it really isn't necessary. Normal savings' accounts in Japan have abysmal interest rates and I think it's because of the expense all of the extra "customer perks" add on.

The no frills banking system in America is a far cry from the full-service attention customers get here in Japan. It is a shame, though, that Japanese banks give such poor interest rates on deposited money, considering that Japan is probably one of the most saving-oriented nations of people in the world. I am sure people would prefer higher yields on their money rather than getting a box of tissue or soap detergent when they visit.

I shouldn't complain too much because there is one area where low interest rates work to the advantage of the Japanese customers—house loans. When I bought my home in Japan, I was pleasantly surprised to learn that my entire house loan was on a fixed rate of only 2.5% (average in Japan). In a country where true bargains are few and far between, this is one area where Japan definitely has the US beat.

The Perils of Learning Japanese

People back home often ask me if Japanese is a hard language to learn. I have to say, without hesitation or equivocation, that "yes", it is. It's not impossible, but it will take some serious studying to master it properly.

When I first arrived to Japan in 1989, I had absolutely no language ability whatsoever. In fact, I had just come from living in Costa Rica, so my Spanish was still very fresh in my mind. I remember being spoken to in those early days and my knee-jerk reaction was to answer the person in Spanish. My brain, at that time, was programmed for Spanish and since Japanese was completely unintelligible to me, I spoke in Spanish; after all, it was a foreign tongue and I had no real Japanese words to spew forth, so often times Spanish would pour out of my mouth without even a second thought. Needless to say, I received a lot of puzzled looks...more than if had I just spoken in English, I'm sure.

This habit soon came to pass as I realized very quickly that having no viable language skills was going to be my biggest hurdle in functioning normally as a member of the community. I think that most people who are studying Japanese would agree with me when I say that speaking Japanese isn't all that difficult—but learning to read and write it, well, that's a whole different story.

The Japanese language uses four different types of syllable systems: *Kanji* (Chinese characters), *hiragana* (Japanese cursive syllables), *katakana* (the Japanese alphabet reserved for writing adopted foreign words), and *romaji* (the Romanized alphabet). In order to be able to read a newspaper, one should be able to read 1,945 basic Chinese characters. This is why it is so difficult to become proficient in reading and writing Japanese in a short amount of time. One needs to study, practice, study more, memorize, and study even more, all of the characters (over and over) in order to master them properly.

Admittedly, I can read a lot more than I can write. But I still cannot pick up a newspaper and read it. My saving grace, thank goodness, is that even Japanese people themselves have difficulty in remembering the more obscure *kanji* sometimes. Often is the case where even common characters will have several readings and each one can change the meaning of the sentence dramatically.

Japanese children first begin by learning *hiragana* (48 syllables) and then *katakana* (another 48 syllables) before embarking on the arduous task of learning the thousands of *kanji* they will eventually need to function in school and society in general. The rote memorization method for learning seems to work well here because Japan has one of the highest literacy rates in the world. This is all the more remarkable when considering it also has one of the most complicated and difficult writing systems in the world.

When I visit home with my Japanese friend who doesn't speak English, my family and friends are always impressed with how fluent my Japanese sounds to their ears. The truth is, Japanese is a very polite language, which makes it a "wordy" sounding language; a lot is seemingly said for a very simple conveyance. For instance, if I were to say "thanks a lot" it could be translated as "*honto ni doomo arigato gozaimashita.*" It seems like a mouthful, but it really isn't…it's just very polite and this politeness takes a lot of extra syllables to make an utterance.

Since I never studied Japanese formally, I tend to make a lot of mistakes. An example of an embarrassing linguistic moment for me was when I was giving a tour of my house for a television program. On camera, live, I said "…and here is my butt." The words for "butt" and "closet" are very close. I quickly corrected myself, but it wasn't quick enough not to be caught on tape.

All of my students noticed it and got a kick out of my struggle with learning their language. All language learners have similar stories of making silly linguistic gaffes. Also, learning a foreign language as an adult is always much harder than learning it as a teenager. To complicate things, living in rural Japan makes the luxury of a professional Japanese teacher to learn from next to impossible to find. But, I am certainly functional and I am definitely communicative which is most important. I can always get my meaning across, and as with any language, one always understands more than one can say.

I am constantly learning and this will never change no matter how much I study and learn. There are purportedly some 20,000 actual Chinese characters in existence. Needless to say, I have a ways to go, but it has been, and continues to be, a very self-satisfying adventure.

What's in a name?

In English, my name has a certain regal or majestic ring to it. My surname, LEONARD, means "strong as a lion" in old English. My given name, TODD, means "cunning or sly like a fox." So, together, my first and family names convey a person who should be crafty or devious yet strong and imposing. Oh, how I wish this were the way that Japanese people interpreted my names!

Since our custom in the United States is to dispense with formality and address people by their first names, I naturally followed this custom when I arrived in Japan. When I first arrived here, people asked me how I wanted to be addressed and I said, "Please call me Todd."

The English pronunciation of the "o" in my name is more like the Japanese vowel "a." From the beginning, however, Japanese people who read my name on paper tended to pronounce it with a *katakana* (Japanese syllabic pronunciation) interpretation. They divided it into the two closest sounding Japanese syllables (which is how they thought it should be pronounced, according to their own linguistic logic). My knowledge of Japanese in those early years was nonexistent, so it didn't occur to me that I should make an effort to correct everyone each time it was pronounced "Toh-doh."

It wasn't until I was introduced to five-hundred anxious junior high school kids at a morning assembly did I realize just how ridiculous my name sounded to a Japanese speaker's ears. When I was introduced by the principal as "TODO-san", the students confusingly and nervously looked at each other, and then began to snicker quietly to themselves. This made me feel very self-conscious as I stared back at 500 pairs of eyes. What is so funny about my name I wondered? Afterwards, I asked a teacher what the deal was with my name and she hesitantly told me that, in Japanese, my name translates to "Mr. Walrus."

No wonder the kids laughed. It's funny. Americans would react similarly to a Japanese name which means something completely different in English. A good example of this is a Japanese friend of mine who is named "Saiko." In English, "Saiko" is pronounced exactly like "psycho," of which good first impressions are not made. To our native ears, it sounds really strange. Appropriately, though, she is married to an American man named "Dave." In Japanese, that is pronounced

"DEBU-san," which means "Mr. Fat Man." So when Dave is in Japan, people are always amused at the sound of his name, and when his wife is in the US, Saiko receives a similar reaction to her name. A match made in heaven.

The pronunciation of Japanese vowels (a, e, i, o, u) is a lot like Spanish. This makes it more difficult for people to say correctly a Japanese person's name because it isn't a part of the linguistic knowledge for most people in the US. Each vowel and syllable is pronounced separately. For instance, the Japanese name Naoko is actually pronounced "Now-ko" and not "Nay-O-ko." It is very hard for people not to mispronounce it because it seems like it should be the way that is most usual to an English speaker's customary way of speaking.

Japanese people have the same problem when trying to pronounce an English name. It is natural for them to say it in syllables, which adds extra vowels to the word; this changes the intended English pronunciation. For instance, the common name "Scott" becomes "SUKOTTO" when pronounced by a Japanese person. It's a variation of the actual pronunciation, an approximation of what they think it should sound like.

I now largely go by my family name, which in Japanese is pronounced "REONARUDO." And yes, inevitably, I receive a lot of wisecracks like "Hey, Da Vinci-san!" or "Mr. Da Vinci, how is your painting going?" Admittedly, being referred to in connection with a noted renaissance artist and inventor is much more appealing than being compared to a massive artic sea mammal. In hindsight, I wish I had researched my names and their meanings in Japanese a bit before deciding on what I wanted to be called. The least problematic and easiest to pronounce for Japanese is my middle name—Jay. It has the same sound in both languages but can mean "nurturer of wisdom" in Japanese which is really quite nice and refreshing. So, what's in a name? A lot, especially when it is being pronounced in a foreign language.

Corn on pizza?

Food traditions in Japan, like in all cultures, are an integral part of its long, and rich, cultural-food history. Perhaps because of Japan's historic isolation for so many centuries, its traditional foods are mostly quite bland, being centered on seafood, rice and soy products. Japan has given the world *suki yaki*, *sushi*, *sashimi*, cup-a-noodle, *shitake* mushrooms, and *tofu*, to name a few.

Of course, Japan's food tradition is not without outside influence. The Japanese, over the centuries, borrowed food traditions from China (ramen noodles), Korea (*kimchi*, hot-spiced fermented cabbage), Portugal (bread) and America (fast food). These foods have become such an engrained part of food-culture in Japan that many Japanese don't realize that they came from outside. Even young people today regard places like McDonald's as being "Japanese" because they have grown up with it.

Curry and rice is also a favorite of Japanese people, and is eaten weekly by most families. Japanese curry, however, has been adjusted to fit Japanese people's tastes. It is not nearly as spicy as curry in Thailand or India.

It is natural when a culture adopts a food from another culture, that it makes it more palatable to the people of that culture. Many Japanese are surprised, for instance, when they visit the US and are offered "California Rolls" (which look like the traditional Japanese *sushi*, but in fact are purely an American invention based on the traditional Japanese food). Authentic Japanese *sushi* can be found in the US, but today many restaurants and food shops are offering *sushi* with an American twist.

Another example is the Japanese steak house that is popular in the United States—where the chefs theatrically slice and dice the meat at the table while twirling the knives in the air. These types of restaurants do not exist in Japan. Many restaurants in Japan do cook the food at the table for the customers, but there is no "knife show." A very clever American-based restaurateur most likely added this showy touch to entertain customers during the dining experience. It worked. Americans love the mini-show at the table and enjoy seeing their food prepared before their eyes.

Practically every culture in the world has its own rendition of the famous Italian pizza pie. Japan is no different. However, pizza in Japan is usually served with a decidedly Japanese flavor.

A favorite pizza topping in Japan is corn. Before being baked, it is sprinkled all over the top. I've gotten so used to this ingredient that I have grown to like it. Now, it seems strange when I return home to find there is no corn on pizzas!

Other ingredients that Japanese often put on their pizzas are: pineapple (to give it that Hawaiian flavor), squid, crab meat, teriyaki chicken, seaweed, curry, shrimp, sliced roast beef, wiener sausages (halved, not sliced); and all of the standard ingredients that we Americans commonly put on our pizzas: pepperoni, sausage, green pepper, onion, etc.

For an afternoon snack, a person in Japan can choose shrimp chips, green tea ice cream, or rice cookies. To wash it down, a variety of drinks are available: Pocari Sweat (not really sweat, but a sports' drink), Calpis (don't worry, it isn't what it sounds like), or canned ice-coffee.

Coca-Cola does a tremendous business in the area of canned coffee. Its big seller is called "Georgia Coffee" and can be purchased from any Coca-Cola vending machine. It can be purchased cold, in the summer, and hot, in the winter.

I had never tasted ice-coffee before moving to Japan. It is consumed here in the summer (much like ice-tea is drank in the United States). Strangely, Coca-Cola has never offered this beverage to its US market. Perhaps they test marketed it and Americans just didn't like it. Japanese people, on the other hand, love it...as do I.

Going to McDonald's, a very American institution, offers the visitor to Japan some rather interesting and unique menu choices that s/he normally wouldn't see in a McDonald's in the US. Of course, the Big Mac, Quarter Pounder with Cheese, and French fries are offered, but in addition one can also order a "Moon Burger" (fried egg on a hamburger patty), *Teriyaki* Burger, *Yaki-Niku Sando* (shredded pork on a burger bun), to name a few.

When there was a scare in the Japanese beef industry with "Mad Cow Disease," Japanese people in great numbers began to shy away from eating beef; to ensure that they didn't lose loyal customers, fast food establishments, like McDonald's, creatively came up with a variety of food items that used chicken, pork, fish and eggs to counteract people's worries.

When I get homesick for American food, I can always pop into McDonald's for a Big Mac, large fries and a coke—hold the fish sauce and seaweed, please. Next time you order a pizza, though, try asking for corn to be put on it. Try it, you might like it.

The Blind Shaman Women of Aomori

Everywhere in Japan, and during every season, festivals are a very visible part of the Japanese landscape. July, however, seems to have more festivals than usual which makes it a very entertaining month. Many neighborhoods have Shinto shrines, and with those come festivals to honor the gods who are kept in the shrine.

Festivals are especially fun for children because they get to don their special festival clothes (summer *kimono* and *geta*—wooden platform shoes), eat lots of decadent foods and sweets, and participate in traditional folk dancing in a big circle.

Festival traditions here remind me a lot of the fairway activities at the county fair; there are lots of food stalls, arcade-like games, and, of course, cotton candy. Japanese children desperately try to win goldfish and stuffed animals, just like American kids do.

Favorite foods here aren't corn dogs or roasted corn-on-the-cob, but grilled eel or squid on a stick. The heat of the summer makes crushed ice deserts (like our snow cones) very popular and tasty treats for both adults and children.

One festival, in particular, that people from all over come to partake in, takes place on the northern most tip of Honshu Island, in Aomori. It is called "Itako no Matsuri," or "The Blind Shaman Festival."

The actual place where this festival is held is Mount Osorezan, a sacred mountain to the people in this area. What makes this mountain so special and distinct is that when you pass across a small bridge linking it to the outside you enter into what is called the "Valley of the Dead." It is here that all of the unsettled souls of those who have passed into Spirit spend their time before moving on into the afterlife.

The natural surroundings have an eerie feeling because of the mountain's secluded location and odd-shaped rocks that jut out in all directions; also, the very pungent smell of sulfur emanating from the bubbling hot springs that flow just below the surface adds a sense of foreboding doom to this area. Enterprising elderly women use these hot springs to boil eggs to sell to visitors. The vapor seeping skyward from the cracks in the earth give this mountain a hellish appearance, worthy of a Hollywood film.

The hundreds of big black crows flying about, squawking and mocking visitors also add to the mystery of this place. These birds are fearless and a bit scary. The crows gather in great numbers here because relatives and friends of those who died visit the mountain to leave offerings of food and drinks to help appease the souls of their loved ones.

Little nooks and crannies, naturally carved out of the side of the mountain, are used as makeshift altars; photos, favorite personal objects, as well as foods and drinks, are reverently placed, along with incense, to the souls of the departed. Small stones are neatly piled in various places around the mountain. I was told by a friend that they were there for the spirits of children to throw at any evil or trickster entities that might try to impede them on their journey into the afterlife.

It is believed that the souls of the dead gather here, and I believe it. There is a natural ghostly appearance to the whole area and a noticeably heavy feeling in the air. And this is precisely why there is a festival here—to make contact with and speak to these disconcerted souls.

The *itako*, or "blind shaman women," act as mediums to give messages to the loved ones of those who have departed the earth plane. It is curious as to why *itako* must be blind from birth, but perhaps, traditionally, it started as a way to involve these women in the community. Traditionally, there were few careers the visually impaired could do.

Their impairment probably makes them more sensitive than sighted people to energy, which helps them to perceive, recognize and connect with disincarnated spirits more easily.

These women apprentice for many years before becoming full-fledged *itako*. Upon initiation, the shaman woman marries a spirit-god in a ceremony where she goes into a trance, allowing the spirit to take over her body. The spirit speaks through her, offering messages to those present. After that, she can give readings to people. The person receiving the reading usually requests a particular person to come and the *itako* allows that person to enter her body to give a message to the loved one. People flock to this festival in order to talk with a loved one through an *itako*.

Japanese people, in general, believe in and often see ghosts. Regularly on TV, there are specials that show ghostly figures caught on film or videotape by ordinary people. As well, there are some programs that serve as poltergeist "sting" operations. In these, the directors set up their cameras in a place where they know an apparition is hanging about and wait to capture it on film. Of course, a fair amount of discernment is necessary when it comes to Japanese TV; there is always the chance of such images being hoaxes, completely fabricated by an over-zealous producer to get ratings, but many are seemingly quite convincing. A flash of light darting across the room where there is no light, or an orb floating in and out of the camera's range from no apparent source.

Especially, though, the *itako* tradition fascinates me. Many years ago, I did see an *itako* in trance giving messages. It was most interesting. Unfortunately, like many of the older traditions, this one is slowly dying out. There just aren't enough young people interested in continuing this unique tradition. Many of the *itako* today are quite elderly, with few young people apprenticing. It is only a matter of time before this tradition will sadly be lost.

A Unique Festival... Believe it or Not?

There is a unique festival in a small village called Shingo, located in northern Japan. Actually, this rural hamlet is home to a somewhat unusual, if not unlikely, legend that is worthy of an entry into *Ripley's Believe it or Not*.

Every year there is a festival held to honor Jesus Christ. This is not unusual because Christian festivals here are rare, but because it is believed by the people of this village that Jesus Christ did not actually die on the cross, but died peacefully there, at the ripe old age of 106, among the rural trappings and green rice paddies of Aomori Prefecture. The legend maintains that it was Jesus' apocryphal brother who was crucified in his place.

After narrowly escaping with his life from the Romans, Jesus returned to Aomori (yes, the story goes that Jesus came to Japan when he was 21 and stayed until he was 33—the mysterious lost years that are noticeably absent in the New Testament of the Bible; he allegedly studied under the direction of a Japanese priest during those years). The route he took was by land, journeying northward and finally across what is called Siberia today, where he crossed the Sea of Japan to settle in northern Japan, permanently. He took the Japanese name Daitenku Taro Jurai, married a local woman and fathered three daughters.

How did this legend get started? It is difficult to say for sure, but even though most people here think it is a bit hard to swallow, there are some curious questions which remain that make some people wonder. For instance, it is documented that the town was once named Herai, which closely resembles the Japanese pronunciation of "Hebrew."

A traditional folk song of Shingo contains the words "Nanyadoyara, Nanyadorasarano, Nanyadoyara" which is absolute gibberish in Japanese, but is said to sound out the words in Hebrew: "I praise your holy name; we will destroy the outsiders and praise your holy name."

On the land of a local farmer, there is a distinct burial mound at the top of a steep hill. A huge cross marks the spot—a tradition whose symbolism is largely lost on the locals—placed there from time immemorial. This is where it is believed that Jesus is buried. Next to him is not his wife, but the brother who was crucified in his place. How this brother's body was eventually transported across continents and buried there, no one knows for sure. They just know that he was renamed "Isukiri."

Supposedly, on this same farmer's ancestral house is a carving that closely resembles a Star of David, again, the symbolism largely lost to the people here. Another odd practice in this town is to make the sign of the cross on a baby's forehead to prevent illness.

Several years ago, when this story was reported in the foreign press by Reuters, it received a lot of skeptical eyebrow raising. However, there are some rather strange customs that seem to be at best quasi-Jewish and quasi-Christian in origin.

This mixing of Jewish tradition and the use of Hebrew, as well as the use of a cross as a burial symbol and making the cross as a blessing of sorts, which is Christian in origin, make this legend all the more difficult to figure out where it came from.

My take on the whole story is that instead of some 2000 years ago, perhaps a bearded foreign missionary passed through some 200 years ago. He tried to evangelize the local people there by telling them about Jesus and the story of his life, which included the crucifixion.

In so doing, the story of Jesus probably became entwined with the life of the foreign missionary as it was told and retold, and eventually the two merged and became one.

After the original foreigner and his immediate family were dead and gone, as well as the people who knew them, the story began to take on a life of its own. Hence, we have the peculiar customs and traditions that are still observed today, probably introduced by this mystery foreigner.

Or was it Jesus? You be the judge. Believe it…or not?

A VERY Big Shrimp!

I can look out of my window and see Mount Iwaki, the inactive volcano that looms majestically over the city where I live. It is lovely. Truly. This volcano has a very distinct cone with three smallish peaks that jut upward into the sky. The people here call it the "Mount Fuji of the North" because of its nearly perfect shape.

A Japanese friend told me once that Iwaki has many faces, and with each season you can see a different facet of its personality. She's right...you can.

Every morning, I look out of my bedroom window and am greeted by this mountain. With each season comes a new and different face—from spring, when the cherry trees are blooming and the snow is melting; through summer when the thick foliage of the trees covering the mountain give it the look of sculpted carpet; to autumn when the mountain changes from a vibrant green to hues of red and yellow; until the middle of winter when its glistening peak is solid white from all of the snow.

The mountain seemingly does have a different personality with each change of season. It sounds corny, but it's true. My personal favorite is winter because it looks so pure and beautiful in its winter coat. Growing up in Indiana, of course, I never had the luxury of being near the mountains or the sea. It never occurred to me that they were something that I would eventually yearn for and come to enjoy so. Perhaps that's why I never take my life in Japan for granted.

Probably people who grow up here don't even notice the mountain...but I do. And I always will because I make a point not to forget how lucky I am to be so near such a spiritually uplifting and proud product of nature.

I'm sure a Japanese person living in the Midwest is equally fascinated with the rolling acres of farmland that look like they extend forever. I suppose it has much to do with the perspective of the person perceiving the place. To me, being around the sea and this mountain is new and exotic which make them all the more special.

Every year, there is a huge festival on this mountain. When I first came to Japan, a Japanese teacher at a school where a Canadian friend taught at, near the base of the mountain, asked if she would like to go there to see a big "shrimp" during this festival. Needless to say, my friend was intrigued, naturally, so she asked the teacher "how big is this shrimp?" As she asked, she motioned with her hands to indicate a half-foot or so. The teacher shook her head and said, "No, it's as big as a house!" Well, now my friend was hooked. She had to see this shrimp the size of a house.

They got into the teacher's car and they drove to where the festival was being held. People were everywhere; food stalls and vendors were selling their goods in full force; dancers were dancing in *yukata* (summer kimono). Everyone was enjoying the carnival-like atmosphere.

After parking, they began to make the trek up the side of the mountain, inching their way through the hoards of people toward this big shrimp. My friend figured it must be rather fantastic to be drawing so much attention. She couldn't, for the life of her, imagine it being organic…it had to be a tacky, orange-painted fiberglass contraption, she reckoned.

They finally arrived to the *tori*, a red Shinto gate. At that moment, the teacher proudly, with a swoop of her hand, said: "See, here's the shrimp." My friend looked at this huge structure before her eyes, paused, and said, "Sensei, that's not a shrimp…that's a 'shrine'." "Oh, yeah, shrimp…shrine…I always confuse those two words," she quickly retorted.

They both had a long hard laugh. Here my friend was expecting some outrageously chintzy tourist trap, and the teacher took her to a wonderfully traditional Shinto shrine. This type of miscommunication can happen in any language, and is common, so having a sense of humor is a necessary part of learning a foreign language and living in a foreign culture.

They put their hands together, clapped three times, and said a prayer to the mountain god according to Shinto tradition. My friend thanked the mountain spirit for giving her the opportunity to experience its beauty; the teacher friend said she prayed that she would master English better.

Telephones

When I first came to Japan in the late eighties, I worked in a typical Japanese-style office. This was a prefectural board of education office and my job was to travel around to schools to assist the Japanese teachers of English with their lessons. Every month, though, I had several days where I would be in the office.

Since this was my first experience at working in Japan, and because everything was new to me, I tended to observe my surroundings and everyone's behavior quite carefully. I made mental notes of customs or behaviors that surprised me.

In particular, I remember a male colleague in my office whose behavior really puzzled me in those days. When someone would call by phone, he would let it ring three, four, or five times before answering it. The telephone was on his desk, and he usually wasn't doing anything too terribly important, so I was curious as to why he let the phone ring several times before answering it.

No one else in the office seemed bothered by it, but it really irked me. Since the majority of the group rules in Japan, I was obviously the only person in the minority, so I accepted it as a personal quirk of this particular person.

One day, when I was relating this story to a Japanese friend about this colleague who refused to answer the phone promptly, he said that he sometimes did the same thing. I was both anxious and curious to hear his reasoning (so I could better understand the situation in my office).

He explained that, especially in governmental offices, if a Japanese office worker answers the phone too quickly, the person on the other end of the line might think the office worker isn't busy and is idly sitting and waiting for the phone to ring. My friend, who works in the city water office, maintained that if a worker lets the phone ring several times before answering it, the person calling will be impressed that s/he was so busy with work that the phone couldn't be promptly answered. It is supposed to convey a tireless work ethic—even if they are sitting and watching the office TV. After all, the person calling can't see what they are doing.

This reasoning fascinated me. An American, on the other hand, would most likely interpret the delay in answering the phone as being inefficient and even lazy. A phone call that is not promptly answered in the US makes the person calling feel as though his/her call is less important than what the person being called is doing at the time. Interestingly, we Americans would have the opposite reaction to and interpretation of the same situation.

The mobile phone revolution that is sweeping the United States is well into its second and third generation here in Japan. The phones here are getting smaller and smaller, but more and more high tech. Not long ago, they were a novelty and people were impressed when a businessman had to take a call on the train. It gave the impression that he was so dedicated to his company, that he would even sacrifice his train ride home in order to continue working.

Today when a phone rings on a train, people either automatically reach in their pockets to check if it's theirs, or they react with an air of annoyance at the disturbance, rather than envy like before. People give dirty looks to the people chatting away in a loud voice, seemingly unaware of the 500 other people standing around them.

Japan is a country inundated with cellular phones. Just about every person, from young to old, carries a portable phone here…except for me. At the university where I teach, as soon as the bell rings, students automatically reach for their phone to check for messages.

A standard feature here is e-mail and voice mail, so students are frantically pushing away the buttons with their thumbs to see what they missed during the time they were in class. Sometimes I catch students sneaking a peek at their messages during class which I frown upon. Students here really are addicted to their phones. And they aren't cheap, either. The average student spends about $80–$100 on phone charges every month.

Recently I read that the younger generation today, in both the US and Japan, use their thumbs as the dominant digit. For anyone older, it was always the index finger which was the most useful to dial a phone, push a button, etc. With the onslaught of computer games and mobile phones today, kids are now using their thumbs like older people use their index fingers. The downside of all of this is that there is a new malady being reported in medical circles—"sore thumb syndrome." This repetitive motion disorder is affecting young people who are using their thumbs to play games and send email messages by cellular phone.

I have a regular phone, fax and e-mail, and I am still a fan of the old fashioned, handwritten note and letter. I may eventually succumb to the convenience that having a phone in my pocket affords, but for the time being I like being out of reach sometimes.

Language Learning

English is not the easiest language to learn, but because of the globalization of English on the Internet, in business and in technology, it is the lingua franca of people from all over the world.

What makes English especially hard is its inconsistency when it comes to grammar rules and pronunciation. There are so many difficult to pronounce words in English that it sometimes causes non-native speakers problems when trying to communicate. One misplaced syllabic stress can change the intended utterance into something completely different.

For instance, when my mother and stepfather visited me, they were taken to a famous lake on the other side of the prefecture by a couple of retired teachers I used to work with. Lake Towada is breathtakingly beautiful in itself, but many Japanese are very keen to park and walk to a statue located on its shore. The statue, actually, is quite disappointing in comparison to the natural view, but it does make for a Kodak moment, so everyone feels obliged to go see it in order to get a picture standing in front of it.

After parking, my mother casually asked how long it would take to get to the statue. Without hesitation, the woman with them said, "50 minutes." Needless to say, my mother was concerned about walking 50 minutes there and then 50 minutes back; she figured, however, that the two women guiding them were her same age, so if they could do it, so could she. Off they went.

After a few minutes, strangely, they arrived at the statue. My mother was relieved to realize that the woman had intended to say that it was a "15" minute walk, but had inadvertently stressed the first syllable of fifteen, which made it sound like "fifty."

These two words, as well as ninety/nineteen; thirty/thirteen; tree/three; sheep/ship; soccer/circle to name a few, are very problematic to pronounce clearly for non-native speakers of English. To compound the situation for a Japanese speaker, the Japanese language doesn't have the "th" sound which makes "thank you" sound like "sank you"; also, the "r" sound is a cross between an "r & l" sound. Many Japanese can't distinguish the difference clearly and often confuse l's and r's when writing.

A famous example of this type of confusion (that is often told here in Japan) was when General Douglas MacArthur was commanding the post-war occupation forces. Elections were being considered and a Japanese group made a huge banner to help persuade the American leader to allow elections to take place. The intended banner was to read "Pray for an Election"; the problem was that the person writing it confused the l's and r's in "pray" and "election." The meaning was completely changed, making this, at best, an odd proclamation to the person it was intended to persuade.

It is a similar dilemma for Americans who are learning Japanese. The language is largely monotone, each syllable receiving equal stress. Of course, intonation is important in Japanese, but pronouncing words for us is difficult because we tend to accent words as if they were in English.

Another problem is that there are many words that are very similar to one another, and it takes a trained, native ear to easily distinguish them. For example, I always confuse the words for "hairdresser" (biyooin) and "hospital" (byooin).

There is a clear and unmistakable difference between the two, and of course a native Japanese speaker can easily distinguish between them when hearing and saying them, but to my non-native ears, coupled with my non-native, Hoosier accent, I am always misunderstood. I get some rather odd responses when I try to say "I went to get my haircut." People respond with "I hope it's not serious...are you OK?"

When I was a senior in high school, my family hosted a Japanese exchange student for a year. It was a wonderful learning experience for all of us. Jun was always having trouble with odd Indiana sayings (i.e. I'm cookin' up a storm!), as well as trying to decipher the sometimes "off-color" slang he picked up from his track team friends.

In particular, I remember he always mispronounced the word "rugged." He wanted to pronounce it like "mugged." I always corrected him, but he maintained that it didn't make any sense why English would have two words so similar in spelling, but so different in pronunciation. Hmmm, it is true. English really is a troublesome language to learn as far as grammar, spelling and pronunciation are concerned.

I suppose that these are the pitfalls of learning a foreign language and with living in a foreign culture: being misunderstood. I do have to say, however, that it is well worth the occasional blunder or miscommunication to experience firsthand the joy of being able to communicate in another language and with the people of that culture. Besides, these linguistic errors make for good stories later on.

O-Bon Season

Every summer, during August, my city hosts the *Neputa* Festival. Huge, fan-shaped floats are pulled down the main street by scores of people dressed in traditional costumes.

This festival, and its sister festival in the prefectural seat of Aomori, the "Nebuta" Festival, are attended by people from all over the country. In fact, this festival is so well-known that if you were to mention it to any Japanese person, s/he would be familiar with it.

Large drums called "taiko" are also pulled and the rhythm of the beating drums keeps the people moving along. The Hirosaki festival is much more subdued than the Aomori festival. The people at our festival, in unison, chant "ya-ya-do" in very slow and methodical voices.

In Aomori, the people pulling the floats work themselves into a frenzy by hopping on one leg, screaming "ra-se-ra, ra-se-ra." The festival attendees scramble for bells that the float-pullers throw into the crowds of people watching from the sidelines. These bells, hanging by strings, are pinned all over the summer kimonos they are wearing. They just tug them free and throw them. Kids especially enjoy collecting as many bells as they can.

The floats themselves, in both festivals, are enormous paper images of legendary characters, brightly painted and meticulously constructed. Contests for the best float occur and companies, schools, and organizations work night and day for weeks in advance to make these spectacular structures come to life. They are done in great secrecy, behind closed doors or are completely shrouded in tents.

This is a nighttime festival, so the floats are lit from inside which make them glow brilliantly against the darkness of the night. It is quite magical. A friend of mine has a pub on the main street where the long procession of floats travel, so I always reserve a window seat on the second floor to sit and watch the floats from a bird's eye view.

I was told that this festival originally started as a way to scare away warring factions who threatened this area. The giant, ominous looking floats of sword-bearing Samurai fighters, coupled with the erratic jumping and screaming of the villagers, were enough to keep the enemy at bay. Hence, the start of this yearly tradition.

In Hirosaki, where I live, the festival is said to have started as a celebration festival to honor the Aomori festival for being so effective. The floats here, albeit gigantic, are not shaped like people, but as big fans. Similar to the other festival, warrior images are painted on one side and the other side always features a goddess.

Another version of the festival's origin relates to purification, and a way to purify the community at summer's end. It was believed to expel bad fortune and to welcome the *O-Bon* season, the time when Japanese console the spirits of their ancestors.

During the time of *O-Bon*, just after dark, small fires dot my neighborhood. For the departed relatives who will be making their way home, people burn kindling wood in front of their homes to light the path. My next door neighbor, a widow, faithfully lights her *O-Bon* fire every night during this period.

When I first moved to my present home, she always had her grandchildren with her to help. They enjoyed the novelty of stoking the fire. Today, they are all grown up and uninterested in continuing this tradition. I, however, find this yearly ritual to be fascinating. I will often sit and chat with her while she performs her familial and religiously based duties.

Interestingly, Japanese light fires to attract the spirits, and in the United States, at Halloween, we make jack-o-lanterns to scare the spirits away. I suppose the spirits we intend to scare away are evil, whereas in Japan they want to assist the spirits of departed loved ones who are making their way home.

This Buddhist tradition was originally observed in China, another country that places great emphasis on ancestral worship. Typically in Japan, families set up a "spirit altar" in front of the family's main Buddhist altar. Here they place special items, such as foods, flowers and drinks as offerings for the departed souls.

When I lived in Tokyo as a 17-year-old exchange student, I got to experience firsthand the entire *O-Bon* festival tradition. A priest was invited to the house to chant a sutra; afterwards, he was treated to a huge feast, with lots of *sake*. Before he arrived, my host mother prepared the favorite foods of the grandparents who had passed and placed all of it on the altar. She also made miniature oxen and horses out of vegetables (using disposable wooden chopsticks for their legs and tails); these were placed there to help transport the ancestors back to the home.

During the actual *O-Bon* holiday we gathered at the oldest son's house, my host mother's elder brother. It was very much like an American-style reunion, except at one point we all walked together to the graveyard and participated in a cleansing ritual where everyone took turns cleaning the family gravestone with water and a brush.

Since all Japanese are cremated, there is usually one large stone for the entire extended family; the ashes of loved ones are often interred there. We lit incense and prayed, then returned to the festivities at the house.

Just like Thanksgiving and Christmas in the US, the holiday seasons of *O-Bon* and New Year's are the two occasions where Japanese will return home no matter how far from their ancestral home they may live.

Contraband in Schools

When I first came to Japan, I was an Assistant Language Teacher assigned to a prefectural board of education office, sponsored by the Ministry of Education. This assignment required that I travel to over twenty different schools throughout the school year, so I tried to rotate my visitations in order to visit all of the schools equally. During my school visits, I often times sat in on the morning teachers' meetings, which offered me a unique glimpse and insight into the daily workings of a Japanese school.

At one such meeting, the atmosphere of the normally cordial and routine gathering of teachers was very tense and even belligerent. Teachers were speaking in raised voices, which was highly irregular for such a meeting. After observing all of this, I decided to ask a teacher sitting next to me about what was being discussed. She hesitantly flipped through her Japanese-English dictionary, wrote a message on a piece of paper, and then carefully slid the folded paper over to me. When I opened and read her note my heart sank. It said: "Some students were found with contraband."

I couldn't believe it—CONTRABAND. Could it be that some of those sweet, bright-eyed, smiling students that I so dearly loved were involved in some rather heavy, even illegal, and perhaps dangerous behavior? As I sat there, I tried to imagine what type of contraband the students were harboring. The teachers continued their lively and boisterous debate and my curiosity finally got the best of me. I had to know what the students had been caught doing.

I wrote a note back to the same teacher who wrote the initial note: "Were students involved in drugs?" She shook her head no. "Were students smoking?" Again, she said no. "Did a student bring a knife, or worse, a gun to school?" Emphatically, she vigorously shook her head no. "What then?" I wrote.

She took the paper and wrote: "Some students smuggled candy, gum, comic books and music CDs into the school. We may have to check the students' bags in…[she quickly flipped through her dictionary] a shakedown to stop this bad behavior."

I just about burst out laughing. Here I had imagined all of the worst possible scenarios, and in fact all of the fuss was over things that most American school kids do regularly. I am sure that American junior high school teachers would be relieved if the only "contraband" they ever found in students' possession could be chewed, eaten, read or listened to via headphones.

Of course, just like everywhere else, this quaint naïveté of Japanese adolescents is changing, and rapidly. More and more students are becoming truant, violent and all around ornery. Granted, it is still not to the point where students have to go through metal detectors to get into school like in some of the big cities in the United States, but a change has definitely occurred.

One big difference between Japan and the United States is the amount of leeway teachers and administrators have here in punishing students. Corporal punishment is alive and well in rural Japan. Japanese parents have even been known to visit schools to ask teachers to punish their children for bad behavior at home. The feeling here is that one bad apple spoils the bunch, so students are made to toe the line.

If a student is caught misbehaving outside of the school by a police officer, it is often the case where the authorities will first call the student's homeroom teacher before calling the parents. Schools take "moral education" very seriously here and rules are rigidly enforced. The result is generally a very ordered, regimented school life.

I hope for the sake of Japan that the "contraband" never becomes as dangerous as that in some American schools. The current situation where I live reminds me of America in the late 1950's. How refreshing. I hope it stays that way.

Uniforms

In Japan, the length of a girl's bangs to the number of pleats in her traditionally fashioned sailor skirt is decided for her and is strictly enforced. I remember quite clearly uniform inspection day when I was teaching at a junior high school. It actually scared me.

Students would line up according to their class in long straight lines and teachers would move about them with fine-toothed combs, checking for missing buttons, improperly tied neck scarves, and non-regulation uniforms and skirt lengths.

Some of the male teachers would suddenly erupt in a fury of loud voices and a stomping of feet when a student was found not to be conforming properly to the uniform rules.

Where I live, still today, nearly two decades later, many schools maintain a strict uniform code. Several schools here still require the boys to wear uniforms styled after the old Prussian military wear, with banded collars and brass buttons. Until several years ago, boys in junior high schools all across Japan were required to shave their heads. This rule is no longer in effect, except within some traditional school sports' clubs.

Even though everyone on the surface looks the same, underneath the uniformed façade, Japanese students are quite individual. I enjoy observing students on the trains to see how they cleverly dodge some of the more stringent rules by imprinting their own sense of style on items that are not strictly regulated. For instance, many high school students reveal certain character traits or personality flairs by the type of book bag they carry, pencil case they use, and type of overcoat they wear.

One trend that swept school kids a few years back were "loose socks." Girls were required to wear white cotton socks, but nothing was mentioned about the size. Girls started wearing these humongous socks that gathered around their ankles, thus creating a very unique fashion statement.

Another example is boys' pants. The boys got around the normal uniform rule by exaggerating the fit of the pants, wearing them so low in the butt that they mimicked the style of popular American "hip-hop" stars. I am sure the teachers were not very pleased with either the girls' or boys' creative interpretation of the rules.

One would think that after graduation from high school and university, Japanese students would be prone to go wild in their way of dressing. This is not the case. Many Japanese office workers, both men and women, opt to dress in uniform-like manners by wearing nondescript blue suits when entering the workforce. It is what is accepted by society, and in many cases, it is what they feel most comfortable wearing.

Recently, educators in the United States have been debating the benefits of adopting uniforms in schools. It is believed by some that many American students spend entirely too much time and effort trying to decide what to buy and wear (not to mention each morning's ritual of trying to decide what to wear for that day). Students sometimes arrive to school inappropriately dressed according to the normal standards of how teachers and administrators think they should be dressed for school.

In addition, students who cannot afford expensive, name-brands are often made to feel inadequate by others, which is a form of bullying. A standard uniform would certainly do away with competition to wear the coolest and priciest clothes. Everyone would be dressed the same.

Since Japanese students are not afforded the opportunity to dress in street clothes at school, they do not feel the same type of pressure that US students feel to try to "out-dress" their peers. Japanese students, however, have other pressures to occupy their time, like entrance examinations and fitting in at all costs.

Of course, the regulations concerning hair and apparel would be very hard to enforce if the US were to adopt rules similar to those in Japan. Americans tend to regard a person's personal style of dress and hair to be unique to that person's character and being; people are encouraged to be creative, and even to stand out. Japanese people, on the other hand, tend to like to blend in to the crowd and not to stand out. A popular Japanese proverb that is used to describe what happens when a person decides to go against the group is: "The nail that sticks out gets hammered down."

I suppose that all the "hammering" Japanese students receive during their lower and upper secondary school years wears them down somewhat. Once they get to a point to where they can break free from the rigidity of school uniforms, they still feel the pressure of society to fit in with the majority. This identification and acceptance by the group is one of the biggest differences between American and Japanese culture.

Perhaps America is too lax and free with personal independence, and Japan a bit too severe in its quest for conformity and order. A balance between the two would be most appropriate for both countries.

Hospital Visits

Going to the doctor in Japan is a lot different than in the US. For one thing, Japanese people go to the hospital at the drop of a hat—even for minor ailments like a cold or 24 hour flu. Americans are more inclined to visit a drugstore in such cases.

The reason why Japanese people run to the doctor for every ache and pain is in part due to the fact that Japan has a socialized insurance system. It is rather inexpensive, per visit, to see a physician in Japan. Of course, overall, each working person pays quite a bit on a monthly basis (divided equally between the employer and employee). This insurance fee is based on one's monthly salary and is automatically taken out. But the actual visit is not so expensive; on average it is about $7.00 per visit.

Because it is relatively cheap to visit a doctor in Japan, people go frequently and they often receive treatments that Americans seldom ever receive in their lives (e.g. IV drips, ultra sounds, etc.). Since hospitals receive subsidies from the governmental insurance scheme, it is to their fiscal benefit then to prescribe a number of medications, and a variety of procedures and treatments for each patient. It brings more money into the hospital.

Once when I had a lower abdomen stomachache, I went to the hospital because the teachers in my school insisted. Immediately, I was laid down and given an IV; later I was given an ultra sound. Nothing was conclusive, and it went away in 48 hours—a common stomach flu probably.

But the type and amount of treatment and the over-prescribing of medication really shocked me. I was given an assortment of pills and powders with no indication of what they were for; even the names of the drugs were omitted from the packaging. I felt it all to be so disconcerting and certainly unnecessary.

I in return shocked them by refusing to take anything without knowing what it was and its intended purpose. This caused a bit of a kafuffle amongst the nursing staff as they scurried about to find out. I honestly think I was the first person to ever question treatment there; something that Americans feel is the right of any patient.

There are certainly a number of advantages to having a socialized medical and insurance system. The most convenient advantage, perhaps, being that I can take my insurance card to any doctor or hospital in Japan and get treatment. It is universally recognized.

Also, this type of system allows for those otherwise not normally able to have an insurance plan to benefit from it. I like it because I know that I will be treated anywhere and at anytime—regardless of where I happen to be at the time I need treatment.

The disadvantages are the long waits to see a doctor and the "in and out" treatment a patient receives. The time a patient spends in the company of the doctor for a diagnosis is very short in comparison to the United States. Japanese patients are expected to dutifully obey the doctor, speaking only when spoken to, and never questioning treatment or asking questions about their illness.

People who go to a hospital are assigned a doctor randomly. This is another disadvantage of the socialized health-care system—the lack of choice in choosing a physician with which one can build a mutual rapport.

Especially, elderly people flock to the hospital as a part of their daily or weekly routine, which is part of the reason why there are such long lines. They will arrive an hour or two before the hospital officially opens to queue up; this has turned into a social gathering where they meet and chat with their "hospital" friends while waiting to see the doctor. There is a running joke in hospitals that if a "regular" patient misses a day, the nurses and doctors worry that she or he is actually sick.

In some ways we are quite spoiled in the US when it comes to medical services. Because hospitals have to be run like companies, much is done to insure customer satisfaction. This is not the case in Japan. Often hospitals affiliated with medical schools, considered to be the best, are drab, dreary and depressing.

On a recent trip back home, I had an opportunity to visit a hospital. I was so impressed with how clean and fresh it looked. The surroundings and décor were very cheerful and conducive to healing.

The average hospital stay in Japan for anyone receiving any type of invasive procedure is 1 month. Even if the person is fully recovered in a week, they are often obliged to stay for a much longer period. This is in stark contrast to the United States where insurance companies want people out as soon as possible—sometimes too soon.

Personally, I avoid going to the hospital if at all possible. I prefer to use alternative and holistic remedies for minor ailments. I just hope that the system can sustain itself because it is in a bit of a crisis now. Many Japanese couples are having fewer children, but people are living longer and longer. This top-heaviness in the system may bankrupt it. I hope not. For all of the disadvantages, and having experienced both systems, I very much like the idea and convenience of the socialized medical system.

The Power of a Simple Act

The time since the horrific terror attacks on 9/11/2001 that took thousands of lives in New York, Washington, and Pennsylvania, has given people around the world time to contemplate and to absorb what actually happened. It has given people a chance to reflect upon their lives in ways they never thought possible...and to learn to appreciate the little things in life—taking nothing for granted. In a certain way, it has been a healing time.

I will never forget what I was doing on that dreadful day. Of course, because Japan is 13 hours ahead of the East coast, my day was winding down and I was preparing for bed. I just happened to flip the TV on to watch a US-based morning show when the first news of the tragedy hit.

My immediate reaction was that it must have been a catastrophic human-error between the pilot and air-traffic control. After all, the World Trade Center towered above New York City, and it was plausible such an accident could happen.

I had called my mother to see if she had the television on yet; as we spoke, I watched the second plane hit the second tower on live TV. I knew then that it was deliberate. America was under attack. Needless to say, I got no sleep that night. I was glued to the TV, as were countless others all over the world.

The shock of it all was certainly felt by the people here. There was a numbness the next day as people tried to go about their daily lives. Many teachers and students offered me their sympathy and asked if I had any friends or family in New York City. Of course, I did, but it was impossible to know if any of them were injured. The "not knowing" aspect was especially hard in the early days.

A teacher friend of mine who works in Tokyo told me that at her university there is a rather odd, retired Japanese professor who is quite eccentric. He has wild hair, an unkempt beard, and his clothes are always rather disheveled. She said that the next morning, after the news of the attack, as he made his way through campus, he drew even more attention than usual. He must have rummaged around in his drawer, I'm sure, and found an old tattered t-shirt emblazoned with "I love NY," the kind with a big red heart in place of the word "love."

This story touched my heart. In his own way, and a big way, he was making a statement of solidarity with the American people. His small, but significant act was simply and effectively done. All who saw him that day knew, without any exchange of words, what he intended by wearing that old faded t-shirt.

Understatement is a trait of the Japanese. Often it is more important what "isn't" said than what "is" said. Reading between the lines is an art form here. Because Japan is such a homogenous nation, people can interpret other people's true intentions through nuance, a look, or a simple gesture. People here know intuitively what other people are thinking, and how they will react to certain situations, without ever discussing it, all because of their cultural and ethnic upbringing.

America, on the other hand, a melting-pot of sorts, is made up of a mosaic of many different cultures from a variety of ethnic traditions; this historical experience makes us a much more verbal people in our daily interactions and associations. Because of the different cultural backgrounds that have come together to make one country, we have learned over time to communicate effectively through speech. Culturally, a look or a gesture may be too difficult to discern otherwise.

Being a foreigner living in the Japanese culture, it is sometimes quite difficult to decipher the true intentions of a person. There are two ways of interacting with others in Japan: *honne* and *tatemae*.

Honne can be characterized as the true intentions and feelings of a person; these are only revealed to family members or very close friends. *Tatemae* is the façade or insincere banter that is exchanged between people in daily life. To state one's true feelings (*honne*) regularly, risking potential conflict with the other person is too great of a consequence for most Japanese to want to attempt it. For the sake of group harmony, or *wa*, people will often hide their true feelings in order to maintain good human relations, opting to relate to others superficially (*tatemae*).

The tragic events of September 11th offered me a very positive insight into Japanese people's souls. Many of my colleagues and students let down their guard to reveal their true, *honne* feelings regarding their hopes, dreams and fears post 9/11. Not a lot of words were exchanged, but I could feel the meaning of their intentions through their actions, nuance and behavior.

The ability of humans to connect deeply after such a tragedy is powerful—and one I have learned crosses cultural boundaries. Just like the man in the t-shirt, actions do speak louder than words.

A Tour of my University

The university where I teach is quite small compared to American universities. With regard to the number of students, it is comparable to a small liberal arts college; the campus itself, however, is quite compact with two main buildings, an annex, library, gymnasium and cafeteria. We also have a missionary house that was built some one-hundred-and-thirty years ago which is now designated as a National Cultural Asset. This building now houses the administrative offices.

Although small in size, it certainly is not insular in scope. We have a variety of course majors in two main faculties which offer students a strong basis in general education. Traditionally, we were a "teacher's college," graduating future educators to teach the Japanese and English languages.

Today, in addition to these and other related majors (e.g. I teach Comparative Culture and Cross-Cultural Understanding), we have a Social Welfare Faculty which prepares students for work in the public sector as civil servants and in private industry as salaried workers.

Hirosaki Gakuin University has a very rich and varied history that started when Japan was first being opened up to Western influence. As alluded to earlier, my university started as a "mission" school. There are many such universities in Japan, those that were created by visiting missionaries who came to evangelize and convert the local people to Christianity. It wasn't too terribly successful as the overall percentage of Christians in Japan is quite low. There are enough believers, though, to support a number of churches in each prefecture.

Although many of the missionaries are no longer here, the basis of their work still continues. Our university is Methodist-based and retains many vestiges of the old days when it was a booming mission school. For instance, we have a charming, gothic-style chapel that has an authentic pipe organ imported from England. The stained glass windows in the chapel are also imported from England and depict many scenes from the life and times of Jesus Christ.

The chapel is very elegant and is a favored venue for couples wishing to have a Christian-style wedding. In fact, when it was built four years ago, it was largely designed for this purpose—a wedding chapel—for former students, as well as the outside public, who wish to have a Christian ceremony.

Every Thursday morning we have a chapel service for students and teachers. Admittedly, the number of practicing Christians can be counted on both hands, but still a goodly number of students attend every week. I think it has to do with the ceremonial aspects of the service, as well as to listen to our university's hand bell choir. For such a small school, the hand bell choir is very good. They perform at graduation and the opening ceremony in April, in addition to the weekly chapel service.

Coincidently, there is a strong historical, Indiana connection to my university and attached high school. One of the early missionaries came from Asbury College (now DePauw University) of Greencastle, in Indiana, not too far where I grew up.

The area where I live is famous for its delicious apples. In fact, many of my students' families are apple farmers. Every fall, students bring me bushels of apples (and bags of home-grown rice) in appreciation for teaching them.

These apples originally came from that early Hoosier missionary, John Ing, who brought the first apple seeds that began this very profitable cottage industry. He is widely known as the "Johnny Apple-seed of Japan."

As you enter the front gates of my university, a long cherry tree-lined promenade takes you past the missionary house. The architectural design of this house incorporated an American or Victorian-style, but was built using traditional Japanese craftsmanship. It is in pristine condition, attracting many tourists who come to see this structure.

At the end of the promenade is the entrance to the main building, which was built in the 1970's when the entire university moved to its present location. Until a few years ago, it was an all women college (which was quite common all over Japan). Today, due to demographic changes and a decrease in population, many of these all-female institutions have gone co-ed in order to survive.

Traditional values and attitudes are hallmarks of the old-style women's colleges. For years, teachers, students and guests were required to take off their shoes and use slippers before entering into the premises. We still have an active PTA, as well as bi-yearly parent/teacher conferences to discuss their children's university work. Many bigger universities have done away with these types of duties, but we continue them out of a sense of tradition.

Living in rural Japan, away from the mega-cities, has given me a unique perspective by experiencing the "real" Japan. The students here are friendly and kind—country kids. Students still greet teachers in the hallway with a deep bow. This appreciation is what makes teaching here worthwhile and satisfying. It makes me feel that I am making a positive difference in their lives.

Education

Education in Japan is markedly different in many respects to education in most Western countries. For the most part, the differences are largely symptomatic of the distinction between Japanese culture and Western cultures. This diversity in culture, traditions and customs serve to reveal many different and interesting aspects of the respective countries' educational systems.

In any country, teaching students academics is only half of the overall teaching load that faces teachers in lower and upper secondary schools. Instructing students on how to live in a global society, based on propriety, is of equal and crucial importance.

It is during these developing years that students must learn how to conduct themselves as active, valued members of society. They must learn how to exhibit proper, socially acceptable behavior in order to function effectively in the "real world" where they will eventually be forced to go.

This is true in both the United States and Japan, but the methods and manners involved to achieve these goals are quite reversed. The ultimate desire, however, is to prepare students for their roles in society; the expectations of educators in both countries, and their efforts to achieve these goals, are very much the same.

Japanese students are basically taught to be "passive" learners, absorbing information that is mainly "factual" in basis. To the contrary, students in the US are mostly "active" learners, being taught to concentrate on the "creative" solution or aspect of the material and to analyze critically the information given to them.

This difference is perhaps why Japanese students have the reputation of being highly disciplined students with a very formal atmosphere in the classroom, while US students are generally regarded as having an informal environment and being less dedicated to their studies.

This perception is not entirely accurate. In fact, a Japanese classroom can appear to be very disorderly with boisterous and loud behavior while the American counterpart can be very attentive, structured and quiet.

Cultural differences help to explain why this is so—in Japan where a group effort is encouraged and is considered the norm, a student who is called upon to give an answer will often elicit responses from other students in order to come to a "group" conclusion. The end result being a chorus of answers being shouted in hushed tones to the student being asked the question. After getting a consensus, she or he then reports the answer.

In the eyes of a Western teacher observing a Japanese classroom, this "group" effort appears to be disruptive and disorderly. In the United States, this behavior would be considered to be cheating and the students would be reprimanded for speaking out of turn and for giving the answer to the student being asked the question.

This Japanese custom of whispering answers is actually very ordered behavior, steeped in tradition that is based on proper social manners. This custom-oriented practice has roots that run very deep into Japanese society and social order; "group" concurrence was learned by today's students through modeling the behavior of their parents, siblings and teachers.

Sharing information (in this case, giving answers) to a member of the group is a very natural response for a Japanese person. A Japanese student would be very hesitant to offer an answer that was not first cleared with a sampling of his/her colleagues. After all, it would be very embarrassing if the answer were to be wrong and very boastful or vainglorious if it were correct. Embarrassment and boastfulness are two traits that Japanese people first try to avoid, and then attempt to play down.

Generally, Japanese students display the tendency not to offer answers or solutions voluntarily, but only when specifically singled out by the teacher or called upon randomly. Even if the student knows the answer, she or he may not offer the answer readily when called upon for several reasons: 1) in order to demonstrate humility and deference by hesitating; 2) for fear of standing out and/or; 3) to wait for the other students around him or her to concur on an answer.

These ploys are the polite, culturally and socially acceptable ways of responding to direct questions which permeate every facet of a student's life. These skills will serve them well later in life when they will be expected to behave according to an unspoken and unwritten code in their professional lives.

It is unfair to say that Japanese children are not allowed to express their own opinions—or worse, they have no personal opinions—as it is to say that US education ignores group membership and the need for factual knowledge. One thing that I have learned from teaching in both cultures is that both traditions, as well as the educational systems which are microcosms of the cultures, *are* different and it is vitally important not to judge the merit of one culture by the other culture's standards.

Educating young minds is the principle goal of each nation, even though each country approaches this goal in a uniquely different fashion.

What's your animal?

Being a city boy myself, born and bred, I am not the most comfortable person around big animals on a farm. Several years ago, however, I asked friends who have a farm and animals in rural Indiana if I could get a picture of me with a cow (wearing an elf hat) for my annual New Year's greeting card. They said yes, and so off I went.

The Japanese follow the Chinese horoscope system with each year representing a different animal. I was born in the year of the "cow," so I thought it would be fun and unique to have a picture taken of me in a Santa hat with a bovine friend.

Well, it turned out to be tougher than I had originally thought. For one thing, the cow scared the dickens out of me. It was much bigger and friskier than I had anticipated. They look so calm and serene from the car window, grazing in the pasture. Up close, and in person, however, they are imposing creatures (especially when you are trying to tie an elf hat on its head).

So, here I was running around the barnyard in the middle of July, with knee-high rubber boots and a Santa hat on, trying to get close enough to this beast to get a photo for my blasted New Year's card.

It was quite the spectacle, indeed. The farmhands had started to gather about to see what in the world this idiot was doing in a Santa hat in the middle of summer. After a lot of maneuvering, and with the artful assistance of the cow's owner, I got the shot.

The tradition of using the Chinese horoscope in Japan goes back thousands of years. In 12-year cycles, the animal for that year adorns nearly all the cards that are sent out. The idea that personality traits can be found in people born in a particular year (as opposed to the Western astrological tradition of signs which roughly cover a month out of the year) is interesting and remarkably accurate.

For instance, people born in the years 1900, 1912, 1936, 1948, 1960, 1972, 1984, or 1996 are "rats." These people tend to be very resourceful, successful, charming and ambitious. Quick tempered, they are quite fussy and frugal, yet generous with those whom they love. Good fortune is in store for those blessed with old age. Rats should marry a dragon, monkey or a cow...but not a horse!

53

The next animal in the cycle is the "cow" (1901, 1913, 1925, 1937, 1949, 1961, 1973, 1985, and 1997). We cows are hardworking, patient, mentally alert, soft-spoken, and inspire confidence in others; on the flip side, we are stubborn, hot-tempered and hate failure. We are rare friends, good listeners, and bewildered by romance. Cows should marry a snake, rooster or rat, but not a horse, dog or sheep person.

"Tigers," who are born in 1902, 1914, 1926, 1938, 1959, 1962, 1974, 1986, or 1998, are courageous, dignified, sympathetic, sensitive and deep thinkers. Unfortunately, they can't make up their minds, are short-tempered and selfish. Tigers are great friends, but unforgiving as a foe. Tigers should have partners who are horses, dragons, or dogs; they should avoid mating with snakes and monkeys.

"Rabbits" (1903, 1915, 1927, 1939, 1951, 1963, 1975, 1987, and 1999) are financially lucky, born gamblers, talented and generally liked because of their nice disposition and eloquence. Rabbits cry easily, are timid and prone to gossip, however. Rabbits are best paired with sheep, pigs or dogs, but are not so compatible with roosters, rats or dragons.

If you were born in the year 1904, 1916, 1928, 1940, 1952, 1964, 1976, 1988, or 2000, then you are a "dragon." These people are aggressive, brave, sensitive, energetic, and are born leaders. Dragons are also the most eccentric. Wealth is theirs in later years. A dragon should be with a rat, snake, monkey, or rooster, but not a cow, rabbit or dog.

"Snakes" are born in the years 1905, 1917, 1929, 1941, 1953, 1965, 1977, 1989, and 2001. Often, they are attractive, wise, compassionate and financially fortunate; but tend to be vain, hate failure and prefer to rely only on their own judgment. Their love life will be happy if they are strong enough to resist temptation of the heart. Snakes are very capable of success and should eventually attain their goals. Cows, cocks or rats make the best partners; but not monkeys, tigers or pigs.

Next on the list is the "horse." People born in the years 1906, 1918, 1930, 1942, 1954, 1966, 1978, 1990 or 2002 are inventive, big thinkers, popular, usually successful and cheerful. At the same time, horses are impatient, strong willed and cannot stick to a project and follow it through. Often, horses are outgoing and popular with others, but tend to talk too much. Success in career-related endeavors comes easily to these people. A horse should marry a tiger, dog or sheep, but not a cow, rabbit or rat.

"Sheep" are people who were born in the years 1907, 1919, 1931, 1943, 1955, 1967, 1979, 1991, or 2003. These people are wise, gentle, deeply religious, considerate to the less fortunate, and talented in the arts. They are also shy, pessimistic at times, and need guidance. A sheep's spiritual connection brings him/her contentment. A sheep should partner with a rabbit, pig or horse, but not a rat, cow, or dog.

Some of my best friends are "monkeys." These people were born in the years 1908, 1920, 1932, 1944, 1956, 1968, 1980, or 1992. Monkeys tend to be skillful with money, extremely active, cheerful, popular, and have a great memory. They can also be hot-blooded, talkative, impatient, showy and erratic. These people have a flair for decision-making in high finance and will go far in developing this talent. Some monkeys tend to underestimate the people around them. A monkey should hook up with a rat or a dragon, but not a snake, pig, or tiger.

"Roosters" are people who were born in the years 1909, 1921, 1933, 1945, 1957, 1969, 1981, or 1993. Roosters are deep thinkers, brave, idealistic, devoted to work, selfish, often tactless, and are loners. Roosters often lack trust in others, yet attract loyal friends. Roosters should watch what they say. It's best for roosters to marry cows, snakes or dragons; but not rats, roosters or rabbits.

Next to last on the list are "dogs." Dogs are people who were born in 1910, 1922, 1934, 1946, 1958, 1970, 1982, or 1994. These people are honest, loyal, chivalrous, good in business and devoted. Dogs have a strong sense of duty, but can be stubborn, critical, a bit selfish, and care very little for social life. Dogs are great secret keepers, and once a secret is in the vault, it stays there which makes them very trustworthy. Although dogs care little for wealth, many achieve prominence. A good match for a dog is a horse, tiger or rabbit; a not so good match is a cow, dragon or sheep.

Finally, the year of the "pig" includes 1911, 1923, 1935, 1947, 1959, 1971, 1983, and 1995. Pigs are loyal, affectionate, kind, courageous, honest and shy. Pigs like to make friends for life, but are quick-tempered, impulsive, dogmatic and single-minded. These people are very kind to loved ones, and have a tendency to be overprotective. It is best for a pig to marry a rabbit or a sheep, but not a monkey, pig or snake.[1]

So there you have it...the 12-cycle Chinese horoscope used in Japan. Of course, some are quite vague, and every type of person is born everyday of the year, but many Asian people follow this horoscope when marrying and when having children. It was reported that the year 2000 had a surge of babies born in Asian countries because it is considered to be very auspicious to be a dragon.

---

1. SOURCE: Information for the various animals adapted from a brochure, circa 1981, L.S. Ayres & Co. Sixth Floor Tea Shop.

In the past, I have been able to finagle pictures for my New Year's card with two piglets, a horse, and a dog, but passed on the snake, dragon, rat and tiger.

Farm Life Tough for Young People

The autumn season in Japan, just as in the US, signals harvest time. Busily, farmers go about bringing in the crops they planted in the spring. Although the crops and procedures to do it are quite different, the ritual is very much the same.

A good American friend of mine here married into a Japanese farming family. Her husband's family farm largely consists of rice paddies, but also has a small apple orchard attached to the property. Although she doesn't do a lot of farm-related work regularly, every year she pitches in to help with rice planting in the spring and harvesting the rice and picking apples in the fall

My American friend asked if I would like to experience a day on a Japanese farm. I jumped at the chance. Even though I don't normally do the "country" thing very well, I figured it would be a worthwhile cross-cultural and learning experience. Besides, many of my students come from farming families, and this was an opportunity for me to understand better their lives and backgrounds.

So several years ago, during rice harvest, I spent a day on their farm. It was back-breaking work, indeed, but I found the entire process fascinating: One person cuts the rice stalks off at the ground; another follows behind gathering them into bundles; the next person then ties the bundles; and the last person stacks the bundles in a criss-cross fashion on tall poles.

My job was to stack them on the poles. There was certainly a technique involved to doing it properly. They had to be stacked in overlapping layers, being held up only by a small piece of wood that was tied with twine onto the lower part of the pole. If they weren't perfectly balanced, the whole thing would tumble down. Her in-laws enjoyed watching the "city" boy fumble around trying to tee-ter-totter these on the pole.

Farming in Japan is definitely a family affair...but it is rapidly becoming a dying tradition among the younger generation. Young Japanese today find the lure of bright lights in the big cities, and a chance to experience life outside the confines of their farms, too tempting to resist. Many young people shun this type of life filled with hard work and long hours by escaping rural Japan to sow their wild oats.

Interestingly, though, these young people often feel obliged to return in the spring and autumn seasons to lend a hand in planting and harvesting. Many of my students from farming families return home on the weekends, and work from dawn until dusk with the rice harvest.

Today, in modern Japan, it is often the case where my students' parents work outside of the farm during the week, leaving the weekly chores to the grandparents to do. This multi-generational system has worked until now, but because of an aging population, and the need to have an income source other than farming, many families are finding it increasingly difficult to continue farming.

The oldest son in Japan is usually saddled with the most responsibility regarding familial obligation—many do return begrudgingly (after leaving for a time to "see the world" and to "find themselves") to take over the farm from their aging parents. They do not return necessarily because they want to, but do so out of a sense of familial duty and obligation.

This son is called *chonan* and is expected, especially in rural areas, to care for his parents in their old-age. The house and farm is generally inherited by the oldest son, and with it comes any debts the farm has.

To compound the problems of a *chonan* son is the fact that he often has trouble attracting a suitable wife. Young Japanese women, who are now educated and more independent than their mothers and grandmothers were, are quite hesitant to take on a life filled with back-breaking work, finicky in-laws, and all of the trappings that living on a Japanese farm entails.

These young women don't just marry the *chonan*, they marry the family. Often, the oldest son and his family move into the family's main farm house and share it with his parents, making it a multi-generational household.

This is not without its problems, however. Many women feel slighted by their mothers-in-law, and vice versa. This friction between these two women puts the *chonan* son in a precarious situation. On one hand, he must respect his mother and yield to her wishes, but on the other, he must make sure that his wife is happy and content in her life on the farm.

Japanese mothers-in-law are notorious for their meanness to daughters-in-law. Perhaps the mothers-in-law, former daughters-in-law, chose to marry *chonan* sons themselves because of the financial stability such a match often incurred, whether it was into a family business or a farm. This security did not come without a price—in this lower position in the family, they were forced to endure hardship and suffering at the hands of their husbands' mothers.

The end result is that this cycle is often repeated when they are in the coveted "mother-in-law position" of the family. Instead of being sympathetic to the daughter-in-law's situation, often times the mother-in-law will repeat the same nastiness she received herself when a newlywed.

These mothers often spoil the eldest son, and treat the daughter-in-law with disdain. Of course, fortunately, I personally know a number of Japanese women who adore their mothers-in-law which may signal a softening of attitude and tradition toward those who marry into the family...but I also know many who detest their mothers-in-law with a passion.

This family in-fighting still occurs rather frequently between the mother and daughter-in-law, both jockeying for position within the family, which is why young women are given pause when courting the oldest son of a farming family. Marrying into such a regimented life, one that may include caring for the in-laws as they age is unappealing to most modern Japanese women.

A few years back the situation in one small farming community was so terrible that the town sponsored a match-making scheme. The whole process was televised nationwide. The town paid for single women to come from the cities to meet young, bachelor men of the town (the ratio of men to women was disproportionately high).

They were all formally introduced, given name tags, and told to mingle; they chatted in small groups, had dinner, and then each man went to his home and waited with his parents. Women who were interested could then visit the home of the man they found attractive or interesting. This portion of the program was in order to allow the young city women an opportunity to check out the "in-laws", the house and farm, and the general day to day living conditions.

Each set of parents put on a huge spread to encourage the young women to consider their son for marriage. It was obvious that a lot of preparation had gone into making the house look just right, ordering the most exquisite *sushi*, and donning their finest clothes.

The reason why they took such drastic measures to attract women to come was that the town's elders (which largely included the parents of these 23–45 aged men) were desperate to bring new blood into the community. Many of the eligible women were leaving—they left and never looked back, marrying city-dwellers to forego the hard life that living on a farm entailed.

The program was a success. Many women were enticed enough to promise marriage. The mothers-in-law were on their best behavior, even welcoming divorced women with children from a previous marriage to come and be a part of their families, something normally frowned upon.

I never saw a follow-up to this, but I often wondered how many of these betrothed couples actually followed through with marriage and how many are still married today. It would be quite a life-style change for sure, because the town was on an isolated island, accessible only by boat.

This type of "match-making" scheme seems strange at best to outsiders. How incomprehensible it seems to meet someone, and in a matter of hours, decide to marry the person without really getting to know him/her.

Not so strange in Japan. There is a long tradition of *omiai* (arranged marriages) and this town just put a modern spin on an old concept. Although rarer today than even just 10 or 15 years ago, arranged marriages still occur in modern Japan. And, of course, with every arranged marriage usually comes with it the ever resilient "mother-in-law."

Vending Machines

Japan is a nation of vending machines. Just about any item imaginable can be purchased from a vending machine somewhere in Japan.

These machines are everywhere…and in the most unlikely of places. I have been on desolate country roads, where out of nowhere there is the bright fluorescent light of a soda vending machine shining out into the night. Nothing around but rice fields.

Japan has been referred to as the vending machine capital of the world, selling anything from candy, soda, ice cream, computer software, rice, audio CDs, batteries, flowers, blank cassettes, panty hose, to beer. Each year I see even more varieties of goods offered in vending machines.

A low rate of vandalism in the streets of Japan is part of the reason why vending machines are so prevalent. Seldom do you hear of a vending machine being robbed or vandalized.

When people visit me in Japan, two aspects in particular surprise them with regard to vending machines. First, they can't believe how prevalent beer vending machines are here. They are everywhere and completely unsupervised (as well as cigarette machines). Although they turn off automatically at 11:00 at night, any under-aged person with any sense would make sure to purchase his/her alcohol before then. Amazingly, teenagers don't really abuse the fact that they can buy alcohol rather freely and unobtrusively.

Second, pornography machines. When I first moved to Japan my mother came to visit and was shocked to see a porno machine outside on the street near where children played. They have mirrored fronts which make seeing the contents during the day impossible, but when dusk comes around, lights come on and everything is in full view.

Also, Japanese people are obsessed with convenience which is why one can find vending machines in the most unusual of places. There are even drive-up vending machines for canned soda where the dispenser is at the same level as the car window, so the driver doesn't have to get out of the car to get a cold…or hot drink.

Many vending machines here have the capacity to serve cold and hot drinks at the same time. In the winter, hot canned coffee and English tea is popular, and can be purchased from the same machine that dispenses cold soda.

Shyness may also explain why vending machines are so popular here. I remember asking a friend why a vending machine selling flowers was next to a flower shop that was open until very late at night. He explained that some men may feel embarrassed to go into the shop to buy flowers for a sweetheart, but wouldn't hesitate to do so anonymously from a vending machine.

I remember reading about a vending machine that sold pearl necklaces that had a similar logic behind it; men who wished to purchase a cheaper string of pearls for a girlfriend may be admonished by the salesclerk for being chintzy.

He wouldn't want to appear to be "cheap" in the salesclerk's eyes, so to avoid any possible confrontation or loss of face, he could easily purchase a suitable pearl necklace out of a vending machine, boxed and wrapped, ready to be delivered…without the hassle of dealing with a pushy salesclerk who might try to sell him a more expensive version.

Perhaps this desire to avoid direct contact is related to the cultural inclination of the Japanese to avoid having to say "no"—for any reason, even to an aggressive salesperson.

Even in a donut shop, if an item is completely gone, the person at the counter will often say, "Chotto nai, desu ne…" which means "We are a little bit out of [what you want]." This, in so many words, means "no" without actually saying it.

This cultural difference is fascinating. Western salespeople often have no problem saying "no." This then probably explains why Japanese people have embraced so strongly the concept of the "convenience" store—to avoid having to ask salespeople for assistance.

Recently, there has been an explosion of convenience stores on the scene in Japan. Literally, every few blocks one can find a 7–11, Circle-K, or Lawson's convenience store. They do a brisk business, and again, are favored venues for shopping even though the cost is higher. A customer can quickly go in and purchase a variety of items and leave rather anonymously. It is clear if the item is available because it's on the shelf in plain view—if it's not there, they are out of it.

The old-style "corner market" has many social considerations to contend with as everyone from the neighborhood gathers there to shop and exchange gossip. As a customer, you are almost expected to stop and chat with the person working there and with those who are shopping. Items are sometimes hard to find, because many things are stored behind the counter.

Young people today prefer to avoid the entanglements that those types of shops force them to deal with: Why are you eating so much junk food? Are you lonely? When will you get married? I saw you with a young lady recently…is she your wife?

I personally prefer the corner shops—prying questions and all. With so much being automated today, I enjoy the familiarity a small local shop affords. It's nice to be recognized and talked to by a salesclerk. I enjoy the social interaction that comes with shopping in a small shop.

Autumn Festivals

Japan is a nation that loves festivals and every season is dotted with numerous festivals honoring Shinto deities, local legends, Buddhist offerings, and a myriad of other occasions to celebrate: planting, harvesting, full moon, children, old people, young people, *ad infintum*.

My city, Hirosaki, hosts a huge autumn festival every year centered on chrysanthemums. The flowers are adorned on huge dolls representing geisha, samurai and other medieval characters. It also showcases a variety of farm products which have been recently harvested. This festival, unlike many of the others, caters to elderly people because it has mostly exhibits and programs featuring traditional instruments and dance.

Most of the autumn festivals originated as a way to celebrate the rice harvest. All over Japan, cities, towns and villages host some type of festival in October or November. Usually, the festival is centered on a local shrine. In fact, these Shinto shrines inspire the bulk of the country's fall festivals.

Shintoism is an animistic religion dating to time immemorial. It is the original pantheistic religion of Japan, honoring a variety of gods and spirits in everyday life. Because Shintoism is so connected to nature and to the spirits residing in trees, mountains, rivers, and crops, many of the autumn festivals celebrate the religious spirit of the Shinto folk faith using rituals that are hundreds of years old.

It is believed that once or twice a year, around planting and harvesting time, the *ujigami*, or local spirit, comes down from its mountain home to bless the fertile fields. The "mountain spirit" then becomes the "rice field spirit" and resides during this time in the local shrine dedicated to this Shinto spirit.

On the actual day of the festival, the spirit takes up residence in a portable shrine called a *mikoshi*. This is a very ornately designed shrine that is carried on long, horizontal poles on the shoulders of the local residents. It is then paraded through the streets.

People crowd all around it, and sing and dance to the beat of drums. The entire crowd is whooped up into a kind of frenzied fervor and people in *yukata* (summer kimono) fill the streets while dancing, singing and playing traditional instruments, like flutes and drums.

Even Tokyo has local festivals. Each neighborhood sponsors a festival around its Shinto shrine. One festival in particular that occurs in early November features miniature good luck bamboo rakes. People purchase these and have them blessed at the shrine in anticipation of the rapidly approaching New Year to help guarantee good luck in the coming year.

When a friend came to visit from home, she was fascinated with these miniature rakes. In fact, she purchased two—not to garner good luck but to use them in her daily chores. Their small size makes them perfect for small clean-up projects. Of course, a Japanese person would most likely be surprised to see one of these *kumade* rakes actually being used. They would use them symbolically, to rake in good luck and to display them in their homes until the New Year.

Another sign of autumn are the smell of baked sweet potatoes wafting through the air. Small trucks slowly drive through neighborhoods and the stove that bakes these have a high pitched, shrill-like whistle sound that alerts people to their presence. High school kids studying for entrance exams in their rooms rush out to get a hot sweet potato as a study-break snack.

These sweet potatoes are not like our Western concept of yams, but are longer and are yellowish in color (not orange). They are peeled and eaten hot, with maybe a dash of salt. The American tradition of eating honeyed yams with marshmallows on top would be too sweet for the average Japanese person to enjoy.

Unlike many American holiday-based festivals like Halloween, Valentine's Day, and Christmas, Japanese traditional festivals have largely avoided the kitschy commercialization that plagues many of our holidays. The majority of the festivals take place exactly as they have for eons with an authenticity that has been passed down through the generations.

7-5-3

One of my favorite days of the year in Japan is November 15. On this day, thousands of little children all over Japan dress in brightly colored silk kimono and *hakuma* (a pleated pant-like garment that boys wear) to visit Shinto shrines.

The festival is actually called *shichi-go-san* (literally seven-five-three) which marks milestone ages in a Japanese child's development. Many couples who have more than one child will have them so that when the oldest is seven, the middle child is five, and the youngest child is three. Of course this isn't always possible, but I know several families whose three children are spaced with two years between each one.

This tradition goes back hundreds of years, but its true origin isn't exactly known. I read once that these celebrations are similar to rites of passage that other cultures observe; in Japan, children were once regarded as "gifts of God" until they turn seven, at which time they become normal human beings. Perhaps that is why the age of seven is significant in Japanese culture.

The age of three marks the first time that a little girl's hair is long enough to be put into a bun; and the age of seven marks the time a little girl receives her first "obi" (a wide sash worn with kimono). The age of five represents the time when little boys receive their first *hakuma*.

This festival is an example of one that was promulgated originally by department stores with the advent of commercialization. Traditionally, this festival was mainly centered in the Tokyo area until modern times when stores began advertising *kimono* and *hakuma* for this special occasion. Quickly, it became a nationwide tradition pushed along by *kimono* makers and children's clothing stores.

In recent years, I have noticed more and more children wearing Western style clothes to visit the Shinto shrine on this day. It is unfortunate, because the charm of seeing the children dressed in their finest Japanese traditional costumes is quite extraordinary.

Today's parents, in these tough economic times, are being more practical. The outfits are very costly and only worn one time really. It makes more sense to buy the children clothes that they can wear for other important occasions, such as the opening ceremony at school, graduation from kindergarten, etc.

The idea behind taking children to a shrine is to thank the Shinto gods for good health, and to ask for future good health, fortune, and success in school.

As one can imagine, this is a great time for grandparents who also get into the act with video cameras rolling, and ordinary and digital cameras clicking away to capture this once in a lifetime ritual. Most Japanese people can show you a photo of themselves at these ages standing stoically in front of the shrine with their parents beside them.

Although November 15 is not a national holiday in Japan, it is widely celebrated and parents get as excited about visiting a shrine to take photos as the children do. It reminds me a little bit like Easter in the United States. Both are religiously based, where children buy special clothes for attending worship services. Although there is no Easter bunny, big baskets of candy, or colored eggs to find hidden about the yard and house, Japanese children do get spoiled with special treats on this day.

In addition to the children dressing up, many mothers wear *kimono* on this day which makes it all the more spectacular. For very special occasions, Japanese women wear *kimono*, but it is rare to see women wearing *kimono* as everyday dress. Of course, a number of elderly women where I live wear *kimono* still and women who work in traditional jobs or in Japanese-style restaurants still wear *kimono*, but it isn't an everyday occurrence to see women dressed in this traditional costume.

Homeroom Teachers and
Guidance Counselors

What are the differences in daily school-life between the US and Japan for junior or senior high school students?

Two differences immediately come to mind: The attitude toward homeroom and the use of guidance counselors. These two areas largely form the basis of a student's school life, which in turn affects an ordinary school day.

Japanese students usually have homeroom twice a day, but for short periods. Whereas "homeroom" in America means little to US students, Japanese students' entire school life revolves around their homeroom and homeroom teacher.

The homeroom teacher in Japan is a very important role model and mentor to Japanese students. The Japanese homeroom teacher takes on the role of advisor, guidance counselor, and acts as the primary disciplinarian to the students assigned to his/her homeroom.

It is largely the duty of the homeroom teacher to see to it that the students under his/her care (throughout the duration of their time in school) develop into moral, respectable, and well-behaved members of society.

Homeroom teachers in Japan who have had incorrigible students have been known to feel personally responsible for the students' lack of discipline and assimilation into the system. They view their wayward students as personal failures, which in most cases is unfair because the teachers did everything in their power to try to get through to the student who is habitually absent, misbehaved, or violent.

The amount of responsibility placed upon homeroom teachers in Japan is related to the powerful influence they wield with not only the students, but also with parents. Japanese parents have been known to call the homeroom teacher to request that she or he punish their child for misbehaving at home. It is well-known in Japan that if a student gets into trouble with the law, the homeroom teacher is called by the police often before the parents are notified.

The homeroom teacher is the focal point of a Japanese student's academic life and is charged with the responsibility of personally developing the student into a responsible citizen. This is quite different from the American model.

The teacher that American students look to for all of their academic and school life needs is their "guidance counselor." Japanese schools, with the exception of metropolitan schools with large student populations, do not actively employ guidance counselors as such.

In my personal observations, though, I have found that many students go to the "school nurse" for not only minor ailments but also to talk in unsanctioned, unofficial rap sessions. Students can often be seen gathering around the nurse's desk in the teacher's room and in the school clinic.

In the majority of US schools, there is a different guidance counselor for each grade who oversees the needs of the students. Primarily, the guidance counselor helps students to decide which courses to take, monitors academic performance, and is there to listen to students who want to talk about personal, family, or school related concerns or problems. In Japan, the homeroom teacher fulfills this role, as well as counseling senior students about their post-secondary plans: career or employment opportunities, vocational or trade schools, college or university options.

Contemporary problems facing the average Japanese teacher today include bullying, teenage suicide, inhalants, violent assault with knives, and self-destructive behavior (especially in the big cities).

For the most part, Japanese homeroom teachers are disinclined to seek out professional help for serious problems because it could make them appear to be weak in the eyes of their colleagues. Unfortunately, preventative measures are rarely taken in Japan and only after a problem arises (like a student commits suicide or is arrested) is the problem fully addressed.

American educators normally do not view the behavior of a particular student to be necessarily related to them or their inability to properly control the situation. Each person is regarded as his/her own entity and free will largely dictate a student's individual actions—good and bad. Hence, US teachers do not usually hesitate to address a concern directly with other teachers, the principal, the guidance counselor or even the parents in order to get to the root of the problem before something irreversible happens.

The pressure placed upon a Japanese homeroom teacher is great. Not only do the teachers have to teach a full load of classes, everyday, but they also have to care for 40 students, including home visits, club activities, PTA obligations, and much more.

Being a teacher in either culture is hard work. Although I teach university, I understand quite well the importance of having quality teachers in the secondary schools—in both Japan and the United States.

Thanksgiving in Japan

I am often asked by friends back home if Japan celebrates Thanksgiving. This question always makes me chuckle, because I immediately remind them of the history of Thanksgiving…no Pilgrims came to Japan to escape religious persecution, and no Native Americans helped them to survive that first long, hard winter.

Of course, this question is asked without thought, and once this simple fact is pointed out, they feel quite silly for having asked it in the first place. I find this to be a common trait of people who have not traveled or lived abroad: Trying to find similarity in their own culture, attitudes, and beliefs with those who are from a different culture or ethnic background.

It is a natural reaction, I suppose, to try to find a point of comparison that one can relate to on a personal basis. The next question I am often asked is, "Well, what *do* you do on Thanksgiving?" My answer is always the same: "I teach my culture seminar classes just like any other Thursday."

Admittedly, it is an odd sensation to work on days in Japan that are traditionally observed holidays in the United States, but I have gotten used to it over the years, and often forget about major holidays celebrated back home.

The only holiday I do refuse to teach on is Christmas. Occasionally, classes are still held up to and past December 25th, so it isn't unusual to be going about my normal day on this very important holiday.

There are two Japanese holidays that are observed in November. The first, on November 3rd, is "Culture Day." When it lands on a Sunday, the following day is designated as "Happy Monday" to allow businesspeople and workers a day off to give them a long weekend.

This custom of allowing a holiday to be celebrated on the closest Monday is a new concept in Japan. Only in recent years has the government designated certain holidays as being minor enough to be celebrated on a date other than the actual day. For instance, the Emperor's birthday is always observed on the actual day, even if it happens to be on a Sunday.

The other November holiday is on November 23rd and it observes the Japanese equivalent of "Labor Day." On these officially designated holidays, people will sometimes display the Japanese flag in front of their houses, on buses and on taxis. Other than these special national holidays, flags are not normally displayed (except for government-related buildings and offices).

The custom of displaying Old Glory in the United States, anywhere and everywhere, is uniquely American. I have lived in several other parts of the world, and the United States is by far the most patriotic place I have ever lived when it comes to the proud display of the nation's flag.

In fact, when friends accompany me on trips to the United States, one of the things they most always notice are the flags that are displayed in front of people's homes, on cars, in businesses, on lapels...just about anywhere! It is a nice custom and it certainly reflects the people's pride for their country which is a mirror into the true soul of the American people.

Although I don't celebrate Thanksgiving on the fourth Thursday of November, I do sometimes get together with other American expatriates and Japanese friends on Labor Day to share in an American-style Thanksgiving feast with many of the trimmings that the average American family enjoys on this traditional and historic holiday.

Of course, a turkey must be ordered special (far in advance) in order for it to arrive in time, and it cannot be too big, as the ovens here are quite small (about the size of a small microwave oven). Pumpkin pie is a nuisance to make because Japanese pumpkins are more like an American squash (small and hard). My dear mother usually slips a can of pumpkin into my birthday parcel which arrives in mid-November.

We often have to fudge a bit on some of the more traditional side-dishes by using Japanese vegetables and sweet-potatoes (nothing like our sweet-potatoes). But the idea, however, behind the feast is very much the same—to share and partake in a bounty of food with family and friends; and to be thankful for all of the blessings afforded to us while living in this most unique and adopted country.

Hollywood Stars Sell-Out in Japan

Often times, visitors to Japan are quite surprised to see so many really big-name, top-rated Hollywood stars peddling cars, beer and detergent on Japanese television commercials.

To be honest, I too was taken aback when I first arrived to Japan nearly a decade and a half ago and saw the likes of Jodie Foster, Madonna, Sylvester Stalone, Leonardo di Caprio, Winona Rider, Sir Anthony Hopkins, and countless others selling everything from shampoo to Japanese *sake* on TV. Today, I barely take notice anymore because it is so commonplace.

Why do these A-List Hollywood actors scurry to Japan every chance they get to do 15 second commercials for consumer goods? In a word...money. And lots of it.

Hollywood actors, who are hot and currently in great demand, can command literally millions of dollars to do a cameo in a Japanese-based television commercial.

In Japan, unlike in America, there is no stigma attached to being in commercials. In fact, all of the Japanese top-name entertainers here actively seek out these lucrative contracts to help boost their careers.

The idea in the United States is that anyone who resorts to having to do a lowly TV commercial is a "has-been" and is professionally finished as an entertainer. I remember as a teenager seeing Klinger from "Mash" selling windows on cable TV and thinking, "How sad, he must really need the money."

Not so in Japan. Here, the general public expects actors and entertainers to appear regularly on TV selling goods, and if they don't, then people assume that they are no longer popular. I liken TV commercials here to being the equivalent of "talk-shows" in America. When a US actor wants to promote his/her new movie, project, book or TV series, s/he makes the rounds of the late-night talk shows to get the word out.

In Japan, this is achieved by appearing in as many commercials as possible around the time the actual movie is released or program is aired. Many hit songs here are first made popular on TV commercials as background music before being purchased by the public. TV commercials allow Japanese entertainers to stay popular and in the lime-light to promote their current project.

I think part of the appeal for Japanese to want to see top-rated Hollywood stars is the exotic aspect stars add to the product's desirability. It makes it more mysterious, more foreign. I seriously doubt whether any of the US stars actually use the product they are hawking, they are just lending their likeness and voice to help the company present it to the consumers.

If these actors so eagerly and regularly appear in commercials in Japan, why don't you see them in the same company's US-based commercials? The answer is that before any big-name star ever agrees to begin shooting a TV ad in Japan, a very lengthy and intricate contract is drawn up. In clear terms, and unambiguous language, the Japanese company is explicitly forbidden from using the same spot in any other market other than the domestic, Japanese one. Probably, the US stars would prefer that their American fans never found out that they "sold out" to the Japanese for huge piles of cold cash.

One memorable commercial that made me laugh starred Dennis Hopper. It featured him receiving a Japanese award with a gift. The gift was a powder used in a hot bath to give a feeling of coolness once one finishes bathing, during the hot summer months.

He was shown enjoying the bath (with the powder) so much that he lost track of time and was late for his movie shoot. The last seen showed him playing with a rubber duck in the bath while hamming it up for the camera. This was in such direct contrast to his "tough guy" image and the Japanese public loved it. It showed a softer, lighter side of Dennis Hopper being silly and childlike.

Often is the case where the US star will only utter one word, like "Toyota." Most commercials here are visual rather than verbal and this is due to the homogenous make-up of Japan. Japanese can infer meaning from nuance and a cultural understanding that comes from being a part of the majority group.

In the United States, the common link between the various ethnic groups is language and the understanding of the verbal aspects of a commercial is more important than the picture; so the visuals are often times secondary to the verbal components. Japan is opposite in that a commercial will use more of a soft-sell, dreamy visual approach as opposed to a hard-sell, verbal approach (which is most common in the United States).

Much can be learned about a culture through its commercials. They often represent current trends, styles, attitudes, and hip language. Certainly, Japanese people learn a lot about Hollywood star-power from the frequent and regular appearances of American entertainers on their commercials.

Comedy Wacky in Japan

Japanese TV, in general, is quite wacky. Many comedy shows use the exact same format. Usually a duo (two men) is the center attraction. Around them, they keep several aspiring comedians at their beck and call. These poor *kohai* (junior) comedians are then forced to do extremely outlandish, and sometimes dangerous, stunts.

The comedy here is borderline slapstick and is often centered on some type of unpleasant or painful stunt or exploit performed on one of the unsuspecting *kohai*. They must endure these humiliations in order to further their careers; eventually when they are the center attraction, they will put their junior comedian troupe members through the same tortuous routines.

I remember watching a program starring a comedian named Beat Takeshi. He is one of the older, more established comedians in Japan and has even moved into films to some extent. He used to have a program where he carried an over-sized fan or plastic hammer to whack people over the head with when they missed a question, said something funnier than him, or failed to perform a stunt properly.

Once he had a sketch called "Human *Shabu-Shabu*." *Shabu-Shabu* is a Japanese delicacy that features thinly sliced beef that is gently dragged with chopsticks, back and forth, through boiling water to cook it. It is eaten at the table using a portable burner and is considered to be quite a treat for most Japanese as it is very expensive.

Anyway, he had a huge caldron with scalding hot water in it; when a junior comedian missed an answer to a quiz he was given (something extremely difficult), Beat Takeshi would release a pulley and dip the person down into this vat of hot water, dragging him back and forth like *Shabu-Shabu*.

The pain and torment was so apparent on the faces of these poor people being dunked and dragged through this hot water that it was difficult to even watch. They were pleading for him to stop, which made him even more sadistic, dragging them even longer. They looked like lobsters when they finally finished the routine.

The audience absolutely loved it. The more pain that was endured, the harder the people laughed. I guess it can be compared to the recent surge in American

TV shows featuring "reality" situations where people are forced to endure the most unpleasant of situations, playing upon their most innate of fears involving snakes, maggots, heights, etc.

Why is that we humans enjoy seeing others in painful and unpleasant situations? Why do we find these things so funny? Is it that we are all sadists beneath the surface, garnering pleasure from the pain of someone else? I don't have the answers to these questions, but I do know that these types of feelings are a part of universal culture, meaning that there is no cultural boundary for such entertainment. The "Three Stooges" are as funny to Japanese people as they are to Americans.

Admittedly, some of the humor on Japanese TV is lost on me. I just don't get it sometimes. As an American, it is difficult to try and decipher this culture's jokes and comedy routines. Don't get me wrong, there is some very funny stuff on Japanese television that as an outsider, peeking in, I can easily understand and find humorous.

For instance, the Japanese have an uncanny knack for poking fun at and personifying a self-deprecating type of humor that stereotypes average housewives, salary men, and students in very funny skits. I guess they are similar to comedy routines that make fun of politicians and the like on American TV.

I'm sure that Japanese people watching an episode of "Mad TV" or "Saturday Night Live" might scratch their heads and wonder where the joke is. Humor is very cultural and sometimes when crossing cultures, the joke is lost.

My father used to say that much can be learned about a person by what s/he finds funny. Oh my, now that's a sobering thought!

Gift Giving in Japan: Seibo

Gift giving in Japan is an art form. All throughout the year, people are given gifts for both formal and informal occasions. One Japanese custom that I especially like is the giving of a small gift when visiting someone's home. This gift doesn't have to be expensive because it is the thought that is appreciated more so than the gift itself. It is a symbolic token of the visitor's appreciation for being allowed to visit or have dinner in the host's home.

A typical gift that is given when visiting someone's home is a small bouquet of flowers, assorted fruits, or a variety of small cakes. If it is a dinner party, often people will come equipped with a bottle of wine to offer. Very rarely does a Japanese person go anywhere without some type of gift-offering in hand.

Between December 13 and 28 people often exchange gifts with one another, especially if they are associates in business or are involved socially. This is called *seibo*. These are elaborately boxed items which sometimes include towels, coffee, cans of fruit, beer, even detergents. Every year stores advertise the more trendy items for that year well in advance of the gift-buying season. They are arranged nicely in boxes, wrapped, and then delivered to the recipient by the store where it was purchased.

This is not a spontaneous gesture of goodwill, but usually a *giri* (obligatory) act. The cost of the gift and quality of the gift usually is related to one's specific economic and social status within the community. People fret over how much to spend and what to buy in these instances in order to avoid any misunderstandings later on because a gift was considered to be too chintzy...or perhaps too expensive (which would be embarrassing if someone gave you a gift considerably more expensive than the one you gave to them).

The custom of *seibo* has been replaced with the idea of exchanging Christmas gifts with the younger generation, an imported custom from the West. Of course, the timing couldn't be better (both occurring at the end of December), and the flexibility offered in exchanging a Christmas gift is much greater than a traditional *seibo* gift.

I tend to panic if someone gives me a traditional *seibo* gift. I feel obliged to go right out and have a *seibo* gift delivered to them of equal value. It seems silly, perhaps, but if I don't return the favor immediately, I may be asked a bigger favor in the future by these people and I want to clear the slate so there is no "obligation" involved.

I have learned this from experience, and realized quickly that Japanese people are very quick to clear the slate. This is in order not to have the pressure of having received an expensive gift without reciprocating it immediately. It seems like a lot of hassle to someone on the outside viewing in, but gift giving is a custom that goes back for centuries and it is the oil that keeps the social etiquette machine running in this country.

Just about any department store, shop, or boutique will offer to box and wrap anything you buy. This is a wonderful custom that I miss when visiting the United States. When I am shopping back home and purchase an item to be given as a gift, I then have to think about wrapping paper, ribbon, and tape in order to make it presentable. In Japan, all of this is done free of charge in appreciation for shopping at the store.

Japanese stores perform this service for the customer because it is an engrained part of Japanese culture, and every salesperson is trained in the traditional art of gift wrapping. The clerks place the object off center on the paper, and then roll the box over and over, with the paper being tucked around it as it is rolled. The end result is an exquisitely wrapped package ready for delivery.

The other formal gift-giving time of the year is *chugen* which occurs in mid-July. Again, this is done more out of a sense of obligation rather than from a feeling of goodwill. The gifts are similar, with all of the same trappings as the end of the year gift tradition.

Historically, these customs most likely originated in China and were occasions to offer gifts to the souls of one's dead ancestors. Over the centuries, however, these have become more and more commercialized and have become a full-blown modern tradition between people of different families or companies rather than an exchange of gifts within one's nuclear family.

Every year I host a Christmas party for my students at a restaurant. This occurs before the winter holidays; we have a nice dinner together and have a Christmas grab-bag. This American custom is especially enjoyed by the students, because everyone gets a gift, and no one has to worry about what kind of a gift to get. The maximum amount allowed is the equivalent of $5.00, and it is anonymous. So, no one has to worry about the appropriateness of the gift or how impressive the gift is. It is much less stressful than worrying about a *seibo* gift.

Christmas in Japan

Believe it or not, Christmas is celebrated in Japan. Of course, it has more to do with Santa Claus, Christmas trees, and presents than the birth of Jesus Christ, but it still vaguely resembles an American-style Christmas in some ways.

One custom that just about every Japanese family participates in is the buying of a "Christmas cake" on Christmas Eve. This is an ornately decorated cake with thick icing, lighted candles, and Santa figurines adorning the top. In fact, it more resembles an American birthday cake than anything else.

Japanese people are often surprised when I tell them that the tradition of eating Christmas cake on Christmas Eve is purely a Japanese custom. Many people assume all Americans rush out on Christmas Eve (like everyone does here) to buy this elaborately decorated cake. This is 100% Japanese.

Where it started is hard to say. I suspect a very clever confectionary owner started the trend by offering a decorated cake to eat on Christmas Eve. However it started, it is here to stay, because most people in Japan now feel like Christmas without a cake would be akin to an American having Thanksgiving without a turkey. It is firmly entrenched into Japanese *Kurisumasu* (Christmas) tradition.

Another very interesting Christmas custom here is eating a bucket of Kentucky Fried Chicken on Christmas Eve. It is amazing how many families here eat KFC on Christmas Eve.

Most likely, a very astute marketing executive for Japan's KFC headquarters started this yearly tradition of eating a bucket of chicken on Christmas Eve via an aggressive (and obviously successful) advertising campaign when KFC first came to Japan. People order their buckets weeks in advance, and line up on the evening of December 24th to pick them up. A friend told me that Japanese people associate eating turkey with Christmas, and since turkey is so hard to come by here, the next best thing is to eat chicken. What could be easier (and tastier) than picking up a bucket of KFC on Christmas Eve?

Again, this is a Japanese custom...not an American custom. My Japanese friends are surprised that as a child I didn't experience KFC on Christmas Eve. They feel as though I missed out on a very traditional part of Christmas.

The TV commercials advertising this phenomenon are really entertaining around this time of year. A little boy in a Santa hat anxiously looks out of the window and is thoroughly delighted when he sees angel-like wings carrying the buckets of chicken to the neighborhood houses. Next of course, after the chicken is eaten, is the arrival of Santa.

Many Japanese fathers put on a pajama-like outfit that comes with a white beard and Santa hat to give presents to their children. There is no illusion that it isn't "papa" who is doing it, because most children here do not believe in Santa in the same way children do in the United States.

For many years I was the official Santa Claus for my city Every year, hundreds of children would visit city hall to have a photo taken with me. I was the only person who had an authentic US made Santa suit, so naturally I was the one who helped out with this task.

The illusion was easier for me to sustain because I was a foreigner and the children were wide-eyed and curious about who and what Santa really was. I dare say that I am featured in more family albums in my adopted Japanese hometown than any foreigner, past or present.

Christmas Eve and Christmas Day are ordinary working days in Japan. The holiday that Japanese celebrate in the same manner that Americans celebrate Christmas is New Year's.

One curious custom in Japan is the idea that Christmas Eve is a day for lovers. Hotels offer overnight packages with four-course French dinners and champagne for young couples to celebrate Christmas Eve in style. This more resembles New Year's Eve for us Americans, as Christmas Eve is family time, where everyone gathers from far and wide to prepare for Christmas Day.

The stores in Japan go a bit crazy in the decoration department in preparation for Christmas. All of the commercialization, fancy dinners, plastic Christmas trees, and the like are not so dissimilar to that of the United States; but the feeling behind all of the glitz and tinsel is.

Having grown up in the Midwest, experiencing Christmas there as a child, offered me a sense of community cheer and family warmth that is certainly lacking here. Of course, the religious aspect was what made Christmas so special, along with the exchanging of gifts, and sharing of seasonal foods with family and friends. The commercialization portion of it was easily overlooked.

But it is not for me to criticize how Japanese people celebrate this adopted holiday. They have their own way of celebrating it that is uniquely Japanese—yes, it was originally adopted from the West, but it has taken on a whole new meaning here that is purely Japanese.

The secular manner in which they celebrate Christmas is not the traditional way I am accustomed to celebrating it, but I can, and do, find a healthy balance between the two. I enjoy attending Midnight Mass on Christmas Eve, as well as eating Christmas cake and Kentucky Fried Chicken. The best of both worlds.

New Year's in Japan

A Japanese New Year more closely resembles an American-style Christmas. This is a time when the nuclear and extended family gathers from far and wide to share in food and to enjoy each other's company.

The exchanging of presents is not a New Year's tradition in Japan in the same way as the exchanging of Christmas presents is in the US. But, Japanese children are given *otoshidama* (a decorated envelope containing money).

Japanese children look forward to this time of year because all of their aunts, uncles, grandparents, and older cousins prepare envelopes of money for them on New Year's Day. This continues all the way through high school (and even college), with the amount gradually increasing each year as the child ages. Some kids save this money; others use it to purchase a special toy or item that they have been wanting during the year.

One year I happened to be in Tokyo on New Year's Eve and Day. I was struck by how quiet it was and how desolate the streets were. All of the transplanted Tokyoites had returned to their hometowns in the countryside to be with their families in order to bring in the New Year. No cars, no buses, no droves of people scurrying to and fro—even the shops were closed. It was all in such stark contrast to how Tokyo normally is—a mega-city teeming with people.

A custom that I enjoy very much is the tradition of visiting a Shinto shrine on New Year's Day. My friends and I usually go shortly after midnight to pray for a healthy and prosperous year. Millions of people, all across Japan, descend upon Shinto shrines during the first few days of the year as a sort of yearly pilgrimage.

Amulets are sold, as well as fortunes on white sheets of paper that are then tied to a tree near the shrine. Students purchase small wooden tablets to write their hopes and wishes upon (usually to pass the entrance exam into either high school or university). These are then hung on a wall near the shrine for good luck.

That same year I happened to be in Tokyo during the New Year, I was taken to Meiji Shrine which is Tokyo's largest and most famous shrine. Literally, hundreds of thousands of people make their way to this shrine on New Year's Day to pray and make a coin offering to the Shinto god. I have never seen more people squeezed into a finite area than at that time.

The forward momentum of the crowd of people carried us, pushing and shoving, to the shrine's entrance. There was no time or space to stop, clap three times, and pray—there was barely enough room to allow me to raise my hand to feebly throw a coin in the slatted box at the front of the shrine.

The near riotous crowd then was shoved and pushed back to the compound entrance where everyone had a collective sigh of relief at being able to breathe again. I am glad I experienced this once, but I prefer bringing in the New Year in Hirosaki, the city where I live. It is much more subdued and although quite crowded with people, it is nothing like that of Tokyo.

My friends and I normally take off for the shrine shortly after midnight. When we arrive, I always feel like I am truly in Japan. The whole feel and atmosphere is pure Japanese: families, young couples, friends and colleagues praying together and bantering about. It is spectacular.

The New Year's holiday usually begins on December 30th and lasts until around January 4th or 5th. A custom that is observed by families, companies, shops and schools is the ritual housecleaning that takes place right before the holidays begin. Everything is thoroughly cleaned, scrubbed, and unwanted items are discarded on the day before the holidays begin so the New Year can be welcomed in with a fresh, clean atmosphere.

Many of the traditional New Year's foods are prepared well in advance of the actual day so everyone can relax and enjoy each other's company. *Mochi*, a thick, gooey rice cake is eaten during this holiday for breakfast, lunch and dinner. Also, *osechi ryori* (traditional finger-foods) are placed in beautiful lacquer-ware boxes that are stacked and brought out during meals throughout the holidays.

On New Year's Day, early in the morning, my doorbell rings every year. Standing there is the postal employee delivering all of my New Year's cards sent by friends and colleagues, neatly bundled. He bows and wishes me a Happy New Year.

This custom of delivering cards on New Year's Day is very important in Japan. Families then pore through them together, reading the greetings and spending the day reminiscing about family, friends, and colleagues.

I wonder if US postal employees would accept spending Christmas Day delivering the entire bunch of cards sent to a family all at once. In Japan, from mid-December, each household's cards are set aside to be delivered all at once on New Year's Day. The postal delivery people then receive the next day off to recuperate from the previous day. Now, that's dedication.

The Fine Art of "Reserve"

There is a very puzzling aspect of Japanese culture which I have slowly become accustomed to over the years called *enryo*.

Enryo can best be translated as "reserve" or the idea that it is courteous to be reticent and to show deference when offered something to eat, drink, a gift, or a place to sit down. It is considered polite initially to refuse such offers, especially by women.

My first experience with this cross-cultural concept happened when I first arrived in Japan. I had invited a group of older ladies to my home for an American-style dinner party.

I had painstakingly prepared everything and even purchased extra *zabuton* (floor cushions) so everyone would have a comfortable place to sit. Today, my home is quite westernized, but in my early years of living in Japan I lived a very traditional Japanese life-style with no furniture or carpet. I had a low table that people sat around, and my floors were covered with *tatami* (straw mat flooring).

When the ladies arrived, I of course gave them each a cushion and asked them to take a seat. Each of the 6 ladies accepted the cushion, but then gingerly laid it on the floor and then proceeded to kneel beside the cushion, not using it to sit on.

Hmmm, this was indeed puzzling behavior to me in those days. I was thoroughly confused as to why they refused to sit on these brand-spanking new *zabuton*. Did they think they were dirty? Was there a cultural faux pas I had committed without realizing it?

Gradually, as the night progressed each lady inched her way onto the cushion. By the end of the evening they were all firmly seated on the cushions (some even sitting with their legs to the side instead of the formal *seiza* or kneeling position). I felt they were finally relaxed and were enjoying themselves.

I had unwittingly witnessed *enryo*, the Japanese art of showing reserve. It would have been perceived by the others in attendance as being rude and unladylike had any one of them quickly accepted my offer of a cushion, and immediately proceeded to sit on it without first hesitating and waiting a socially acceptable amount of time before doing so.

So much of Japanese culture and etiquette focuses on proper protocol and behavior that it is sometimes hard for an outsider to know what is correct and what is not. Of course, every Japanese person from early childhood has been trained in this knowledge and is keenly aware of his or her place within the social structure.

Japanese are very easily offended if a breach of protocol occurs. I remember a Japanese friend of mine who had invited a colleague and his wife for dinner. The host was single, so the only woman there was the guest's wife. After dinner, it is customary that if a woman is among the guests visiting a single man's home for dinner, that she offer to help clean up the kitchen. The offer may be refused, but it is proper to do so as a gesture.

This woman not only failed to offer to help with the cleanup, but she asked for an ashtray and was the only person who was smoking. Of course, my friend said nothing at the time and put on a "happy" face, but later I got an ear full about how rude his colleague's wife had behaved. She failed to demonstrate proper reserve or *enryo* in his estimation.

Another type of *enryo* that is actually rather quaint is the polite refusal of gifts. Often when I am away on trips, my next door neighbor will sweep my walk, water my flowers, and generally keep an eye on my house and property.

I feel obliged, then, to bring her back a memento from wherever I have been as a thank you for her kindness and help. Each time, though, we go through an ancient Japanese ritual of deference.

I first offer the gift—she politely refuses. I then insist, explaining how helpful she has been and how appreciative I am—she refuses again, waving her hand back and forth politely. The third time I offer the gift, I do so with both hands, my head bowed low and say "honto, dozo" (really, please take it), and wait. The third time is always charm, because she then accepts it, thanking me profusely and apologizing that she has made me worry during my trip and for being so much trouble.

It would have been rude for her to accept it immediately because it would make her appear to be unreserved. From my American cultural perspective, it would be rude to refuse (even politely) a gift, a chair to sit down on, food, or a drink that was offered or served to me. Even if it was something that I hated, I would at least taste it in order to show some interest and appreciation for the offering.

This is my American cultural background shining through. A Japanese person may interpret immediate acceptance of an offering as being too forward. By first refusing, it portrays humility and the desire not to be any trouble to the person offering.

I am used to this aspect of Japanese culture, and expect people first to defer or refuse politely, then eventually accept whatever it is I am offering. But in a time-frame that is culturally acceptable to them. I do, however, still tend to accept an offering immediately even after living here for so many years. I guess the old adage is true: You can take the boy out of America, but you can't take the America out of the boy.

The First Customer of the Morning

Department stores in Japan take the concept of elegance and politeness to new heights in pampering everyday customers. Every morning, at exactly 10:00 am, customers are welcomed into the front doors of the department store by the entire staff who line up on both sides of the main aisle to bow and greet the first customers of the day. Each employee is meticulously groomed; women in matching uniforms (sometimes with hats) and men in dark suits and ties.

It is a nice detail that Japanese department stores afford to their valued customers, and one that visitors and tourists to Japan find very pleasant being the first customer of the morning. In addition, every escalator and elevator has a person waiting to welcome the first customers who use these modes of transport in the stores.

In fact, really swanky department stores still employ elevator women in uniforms to press the buttons for the customers and to hold open the doors at each floor for the people getting on and off.

It is actually unnecessary, as anyone who has ventured out into civilized society in the past 30 years knows very well how to operate an elevator, but the human touch these women offer to the customers really makes it special and unique. It is quite nice to be greeted with a pleasant "good morning" and be taken to where you need to go by someone who is courteous and friendly.

These women undergo vigorous training and are thoroughly educated in the fine art of "extreme politeness." Their language, gestures, voice (diction and intonation) and appearance are all carefully honed through training in order to be exactly the same.

The overtly feminine mannerisms and gestures of these women are their trademark—gently motioning with their hands, bowing and smiling to the customers in their neatly pressed uniforms, with white gloves and hats, all serve to fascinate the first time visitor to Japan. Even the men who work directly with the public in other types of positions behave similarly.

As a small child, I remember shopping with my mother on her day off at a department store in the downtown of my hometown. I was always so intrigued by the elevator, and the kind woman who sat on a stool next to the panel of buttons, whisking her passengers to each floor.

In those days, elevators were few and far between, so it was only on jaunts to this store did I get to experience the thrill of riding in an elevator. How easily pleased and entertained I was. Of course, children today view elevators as so commonplace that there is no special meaning in getting to ride in one. It seems like so much more is needed in today's society to entertain children nowadays. Progress and nostalgia go hand in hand I suppose. For me, though, riding an elevator at this store was a real treat, permanently embedded in my childhood memories.

Japan, albeit modern and worldly in many ways, still adheres to many traditions that have fallen to the wayside in the United States. It is so nice to shop at a department store and be treated with respect and honor…the way customers should be. It is a refreshing change to be pampered and valued.

American stores use the phrases of "the customer is always right" and "the customer comes first" as battle cries for good business, but I think they could learn a thing or two from their Japanese counterparts. I have noticed on recent trips home how curt and sharp salesclerks can be in the US. Even the trademark "greeters" at well-known super-stores aren't always the most pleasant people in the world to come into contact with.

Admittedly, I have been spoiled living in Japan, and I sometimes experience "reverse culture shock" when shopping in the US. I expect, and even demand, to be treated with respect. After all, it is in part my money that goes toward paying the salaries of the staff in the store. Without the paying customers, there would be no store.

Gasoline Stations

One thing I hate to do is to pump gas. Especially in the winter, when it's cold and snowy, getting out of your warm vehicle to stand in the biting wind to fill the tank of the car is so unpleasant. What ever happened to the full-service filling station? They are a dying breed, for sure.

In Japan, the opposite is true. The majority of the gas stations in Japan are still full-service stations. A few years ago, the law in Japan was changed to allow self-serve stations to operate, but they haven't really taken off yet. Before, it was illegal in Japan to pump your own gas; only trained personal were allowed to do so because it was considered to be hazardous. Eventually, self-service stations will become the norm in Japan, just as they have in the United States.

Of course, self-serve stations are the norm in the US today. A few traditional full-service stations exist here and there, but for the most part, most Americans have to pump their own gas.

Japanese gasoline stations can be found in just about any space large enough to pull a few cars into. The typical gas station has a roof covering the area like that of those in the US, but from the roof hangs the gas hoses. The customer pulls up under a hose, directed by an attendant, and the hose is then pulled down to the car. Because land is so expensive here, it is definitely a valuable space saver.

As the gas is being pumped, some stations have a system where the customer is invited inside the station to a waiting area. Coffee is provided, as well as magazines for the person to enjoy while waiting. Several attendants then descend upon the car and wash the windows, empty the ashtrays, and lightly vacuum the floorboards. They work so quickly that one barely has enough time to drink a cup of coffee, let alone read a magazine.

After all of this is finished, the attendants stand beside the car and bow to the customer as the car pulls away. Another attendant is waiting at the street to stop traffic to allow the customer out onto the street. This attendant ventures out into the middle of the street, removes his/her matching hat from the station's uniform, and bows deeply to the customer leaving. S/he then turns to the cars that were made to wait in each direction, and bows deeply to these people.

It is quite an experience to go to a gasoline station in Japan. When my mother visited she quite enjoyed all of this individualized attention, because like me, she also hates the idea of pumping her own gas. She mentioned how she wished these types of stations still existed in the US.

The downside to all of the individualized attention a customer receives is, of course, the cost. Gasoline in Japan is much more expensive than in the US, and it is sold in liters, which is a much smaller quantity than a gallon.

The average cost per liter of gasoline in Japan is 40 yen (33 cents), but the government adds a 60 yen tax to that, and then there is a 5% consumption tax that is added onto that. The total cost per liter is about 105 yen (86 cents). Roughly there are around 3.7 liters to a gallon, so the equivalent of a gallon of gas in Japan costs around $3.50.

When I first arrived in Japan, I was fascinated with the average car wash. A Japanese car wash is much more compact than those in the United States. It consists of a movable contraption on a track that glides over the car (rather than the car being guided through a garage type of structure).

The car pulls up to the car wash, the driver gets out, and then it moves slowly over the top of the car, washing and drying the car. This also saves a lot of space, which is very necessary in Japan. These types of car washes are just now beginning to be used in the US. It certainly does make sense as far as cost is concerned. Buying the plot of land and building the structure can be quite costly.

Japanese industry is very inventive when it comes to taking a proven concept and improving upon it to fit the needs of the people here. A story here about just this type of innovation features the founder of Sony. He asked his engineers and designers to come up with a radio/tape player that was small and light enough that his grandchildren could use it. That small radio/tape player became a world phenomenon: the Walkman…and the rest is history.

Automobiles

I don't have a car in Japan, nor do I really need or want one. In my opinion, cars in Japan are money pits that never really pay off. In Japan, cars are required to have an inspection depending upon how old the car is. The older the car, the more frequently it is required to be inspected.

A new car has a three-year grace period where the owner doesn't have to have it inspected. At the three-year mark, there is a mandatory inspection called *shaken*. This can cost anywhere between 100,000–150,000 yen ($833–$1,250) depending upon the size of the engine. The majority of this cost is a tax that goes to the government, with the upkeep portion of the charge being minimal.

After the three-year inspection, car owners then have to do this every two-years, and it gradually gets more expensive as the car ages. People here trade cars frequently, usually after three-years, to avoid paying the *shaken*. I have been given—outright—a number of cars for my taking because trade-ins and used cars are not that popular here. I have no desire to be tied down to this system, so I always pass on these offers. People want to get rid of the cars before the inspection fee is due to be paid.

My first car was a '65 Mustang that I bought used off my brother, who had bought it used off someone else. I am sure it is still being driven somewhere around my hometown still today. The point is many of the cars that are junked in Japan are still perfectly usable and drivable. It's a shame that they have such a short life-span here.

One use for an older car is to use it as a tool box. Rice paddies here are dotted with cars that are parked in the center of several rice fields. The farmers take their old cars or trucks and use them to store equipment that is needed for planting and harvesting. They can be securely locked, and are waterproof, so they make a good portable storage shed. I guess it is better than being put in some scrap yard. Japan really doesn't have a lot of room for junking cars, and it is expensive to have a car taken off your hands.

Several years ago there was a crackdown around Narita Airport in Tokyo because people would drive their cars to an overflow parking area and just abandon them. This was a huge problem for the community of Narita because the local government then had to incur the cost of getting rid of them.

Why don't Japanese high school students drive these old family cars rather than just junking them? Well, the driving age in Japan is 18, and the cost to go to driving school is around $2,000. Often, university students take part-time jobs to save enough money in order to attend driving school. And the high inspection costs make it difficult for a struggling student to pay. It really is a vicious cycle.

American teenagers are quite fortunate to have driver's-ed in school and to be able to buy a car for a reasonable price to drive around in, and at such a young age. Many countries don't allow people to drive until they are officially adults, whether that is 18 years of age or older.

Another problem about owning a car in Japan is where to park it. Especially in big cities, there is limited space in which to park cars, and when a spot is found, it is quite expensive. Even in my small city, it can cost between $50–$100 a month to park your car.

In my old apartment, I wanted to have a parking space so if anyone came to visit they would have a place to park. The fact I rented an apartment there didn't guarantee me a spot. I decided not to because of the exorbitant cost involved.

A friend of mine in Tokyo was so excited to get a car to drive on the weekends; during the week, of course, everyone goes to and from work by train and subway. Tokyo could never accommodate the millions of workers who pour into the metropolis to be driving vehicles.

This friend though had to take a 30 minute train ride to get to the car, because there was absolutely no parking space available near his apartment. So a drive with the family in the car meant schlepping the kids, toys, and any other articles they need on the train to get to the car to fight the traffic to get to the countryside to take a leisurely drive.

Be thankful that in most places in America taking a drive in the country is as easy as going to the market. Give your car a thank you pat next time you drive for being so convenient and economical. Where would Americans be without their cars?

Devil be Gone!

Just like in the United States, Japan has some very long and curious traditions. I'm sure that foreign visitors to the US on Halloween night might be a bit taken aback by all the goblins, witches and ghosts demanding candy at neighbors' doors—no treat means a trick, which everyone wants to avoid.

There is no equivalent holiday in Japan to Halloween, but one that sort of resembles it occurs at the beginning of February and is a favorite among Japanese children. It is called *setsubun* and literally means "division between the two seasons." According to the lunar calendar, this holiday officially marks the end of winter.

Curiously, the American celebration of "Ground Hog's Day" is marginally related to this Japanese holiday, but not to "end" winter as much as to predict whether there will be 6 more weeks of it. It's not an exact science in America, but it is fun to watch the official ground hog run around a pen to see if the sun casts a shadow on him or not.

I always know when this time of the year is approaching because supermarkets build huge displays of roasted soybeans and peanuts. The purpose of the beans and peanuts is to scatter them about the home, inside and out, as a traditional ritual to expel *oni* (devils), and to usher in good luck.

The same supermarket' displays also include *oni* masks that fathers don on the appointed day so their children can throw beans at them, symbolic of driving away any demons that might have taken refuge in the house during the winter. The *oni* is a red-faced demon with short horns protruding out of its forehead, sharp fang-like teeth, and a tuft of black, curly hair on its head.

Kindergarten children all over Japan make these masks at school at the end of January in preparation for the big event. Usually a news crew captures the children being chased around the school yard by a teacher dressed as an *oni*. The kids are running and screaming, all the while feverishly pelting him with handfuls of beans. They are crying and laughing at the same time, enjoying being scared.

Since I live in rural Japan, this custom is still practiced by many people here. Of course, just like many old traditions, this one has faded somewhat in recent times (especially in big cities). I don't think it will entirely disappear because children look forward to messing up the house by casting beans all around.

Of course, Japanese parents have the task of cleaning up the mess the next day, and probably for many months to come the stray bean or peanut can be found lurking in the corners, under chairs, behind the TV and even lodged in a sofa cushion or two.

My first encounter with *setsubun* was when a friend visited and gave me roasted soy beans the first year I lived in Japan. I figured they were for eating, but he explained that we had a set procedure we had to follow: In the evening, after dark, it is necessary to cast a handful of beans out the front door shouting *Oni wa soto*! (Out with the devil!).

This is repeated in every room of the house, shouting *Fuku wa uchi*! (In with good luck!). To be on the safe side, it's best to do both several times just to make sure.

At the end of the ritual, each person is supposed to eat his/her age in beans (fresh ones that haven't been scattered).

Famous celebrities are often invited to temples and shrines all over Japan to do *mamemaki* (bean-scattering). I remember Cyndi Lauper came one year to participate in a planned bean-throwing event. People flock to the temples to be showered with *fukumame* (lucky beans). It is believed that if you are hit with a lucky bean you will have good health in the coming year.

Just as in the case of the United States, Japan is rapidly depending upon foreign imports of even traditionally based items. I was surprised this past year to notice that the package of beans in the supermarket near my house read: MADE IN CHINA. Perhaps I shouldn't have been so surprised; after all, this colorful custom actually originated in China and was borrowed by Japan many centuries ago.

Heated Toilet Seats Standard in Northern Japan

Winter in northern Japan is harsh. The area where I live is called "Tohoku"; this section of Japan is comprised of the top 1/3 of the Japanese main island of Honshu. It is also known as "snow country" because this area is notorious for receiving heaps upon heaps of snow.

People back home can't believe it when I say, "Well we got nearly a foot of snow today…and the weather forecast says we will get another foot or so tomorrow." It seems unbelievable, but this is just a part of life here.

One question I always get is "where does it all go?" That's a good question, and I honestly don't know. It just gets pushed aside, and packed down. My street is much too narrow for a snowplow to come through, so it is up to all of us to get out first thing in the morning and shovel the area in front of our homes.

My neighbors, mostly the wives, are out with shovels in hand to do the daily *yuki kaki* (shoveling ritual). I actually quite enjoy it. This is the time when everyone gathers around to have an *ido bata kaigi* (literally "a gossip session around the well"). So many interesting tidbits can be learned during these impromptu morning neighborhood meetings. And besides, if I am there, they can't talk about *me*!

The narrow road in front of my house has a cement block fence lining it. Every year the packed snow reaches the top of this fence; but cars still teeter-totter on top of it and plow right on through.

In fact, even matchbox like cars that seem too feeble to drive in normal weather just plug on through also. All cars in this area have at least front-wheel drive, even the smallest of compact cars. People here are fearless and just charge on through as if the snow wasn't there.

There is no concept of a "snow day" here. Everyone just gets up and goes about their daily lives—snow or no snow. I have never had anything canceled in all the years I have lived here due to excess snow. Perhaps this in part due to the fact that Japanese people, including students, are responsible for finding their own ways to work and school. Issues of liability in America have made it too costly (from a legal standpoint) not to cancel work or school if the weather is sufficiently severe; an accident involving a school bus on a snowy day could precipitate a slew of lawsuits from disgruntled parents. Students in Japan are either driven by their parents, walk, ride personal bicycles or take public transportation; there is no widespread use of "school buses" in Japan, nor is there a penchant to sue at the drop of a hat.

The snow does offer other dangers, especially when it warms up just a little bit. The snow can go flying off the roof in one huge avalanche and anyone standing under it can get covered. Sadly, every year I read about children who are killed by falling snow.

I have special "snow-stoppers" attached (every foot or so) to the main part of my roof; these are small, flat objects that protrude straight up which keeps the snow from coming off in one big chunk.

The problem, though, is that the snow accumulates so much that I have to hire men to go up and push it off. The doors to the upstairs' bedrooms of my house begin to stick from the weight of the snow pushing down on the frame of the house. This is when I know it's time to have the snow removed!

Admittedly, I do miss central heating probably more than any other luxury. Where I live in Japan, it is too inefficient to heat an entire house, so only the rooms that people are in get heated. Newer homes are installing "heated flooring" which is nice, but if one part of it goes bad, then the whole floor has to be taken up to be repaired.

So, is my house cold? YES! I can see my breath inside. When I lived in an apartment, it was so cold that I had to put all of the liquids in the refrigerator to keep them from freezing. Now, each night I have to do *mizu nuki* (drain the water from the pipes) in order to avoid having them burst during the night.

Because of earthquakes, I must turn the heat off when I am not at home or when sleeping at night. A powerful jolt could topple the kerosene heater and potentially start a fire. Fire is a constant fear of people in Japan. The wooden structure of homes offers flexibility during earthquakes, but burn quickly in a fire. In the old days, they used to have a man go around each neighborhood with two blocks of wood, clanging them together, to remind people to turn off their stoves and to put out their cooking fires for the night in order to avoid having a stove catch fire and spreading to nearby homes.

It all sounds dreadful I know, but I have adapted and it doesn't bother me. I have learned to sleep without heat on at night; I have adjusted to only using heat in the room I am in; and I shovel snow as a part of my daily routine. I figure the people living north of me in Hokkaido have it much worse.

One saving grace, however, is that it is a standard feature for toilets here to have heated seats. This is not an extravagant luxury—it is a necessity. I don't know why some enterprising person with a savvy business sense hasn't started exporting these to the US. I am certain they would be a hit. Once you have experienced the joy of a heated toilet seat, you'll never be satisfied with an ordinary toilet seat again!

Gaman or the Idea of Perseverance in Japan

Japanese people have *gaman* (patience and perseverance). This term is used to refer to people who are faced with a difficult task or problem, or to encourage athletes to do their best. It is a term that is so widely used in Japan that even a casual visitor will notice it and wonder what it means.

When I first came to Japan, I remember how impressed I was when I attended a junior high school's morning assembly. All of the students stood at attention in their assigned spots, concentrating intently on the speaker at the podium—no matter how boring or uninteresting it may have been.

The respect, patience and personal discipline students demonstrate during these gatherings are remarkable. This restraint is also exhibited by Japanese students at meetings, speeches, lectures and long performances. This can all be attributed to having *gaman*—the ability to endure patiently an unpleasant situation. And it is something that Japanese children learn from a very early age.

I often try to imagine how American young people would behave in similar situations. I have a feeling that there would be a lot of sighing, eyes rolling and fidgeting going on. I have seen Japanese students listen to their peers giving speeches for three hours straight with no breaks in between speakers, with little to no elbowroom.

I am afraid that American students would rebel and the teachers would spend most of their time trying to keep them quiet and in their seats. Unless the subject matter is riveting, fun or entertaining, then it is difficult to keep American young people engaged for more than a few minutes. Their Japanese counterparts seemingly remain undaunted through the driest of ceremonies.

One memorable example I have of Japanese *gaman* and American "impatience" was when I was a high school student. My family hosted a Japanese exchange student, Jun, for a year home-stay.

Jun and I, along with several of our classmates went to a special candlelight church service around Christmas to watch another friend sing a solo in the church choir. Early on in the service they had the special performance that we wanted to see, so we were ready to go…but we were stuck in the middle of the pew and couldn't leave. There was an exceptionally long sermon, so we were stuck in our seats for over an hour, with no way to escape.

Needless to say, it wasn't long before my American friends and I were restless, fidgety and bored. We were rolling our eyes and complaining in whispers about how hard the seats were, how hot it was, and how cold it was. We were just downright mad.

I happened to glance over at Jun and he was sitting perfectly still, back straight, hands folded with his full and undivided attention directed toward the pastor in the pulpit. I on the other hand was barely surviving, almost dead from boredom.

The moment it was over we raced outside, jumped in my car and sped off to a local pizzeria. Later, after cruising around the obligatory hot spots, we arrived home where my mother was still up and about.

She asked Jun how he enjoyed the evening's church service and he replied rather matter-of-factly, "it was very boring but it couldn't be helped." Aha! He was bored too, but I couldn't believe how he could sit so stoically without even a hint of ennui.

His actions didn't make much sense to me then, but I certainly understand them now as I have had to learn to acquire *gaman* to make certain situations bearable. Japanese people believe that some situations are beyond one's control and just have to be endured. They maintain that there is no use in fighting them because it is sometimes better to accept and endure the unpleasantness until it passes.

Fortunately, I have matured a great deal since my high school years and I now realize as an adult that we Americans, too, have a kind of *gaman*. Perhaps it isn't on the same level as Japanese *gaman*, but it is there nonetheless.

There have been many times in my life that I have been in situations where, yes, it is better to endure something because it just "can't be helped." Now that I have lived in Japan for an extended period, I have become more attuned to Japanese *gaman* and more conscious of my own form of *gaman*.

I am constantly honing it and always will, I suppose. I only wish I had learned the idea of Japanese *gaman* as a child. A little *gaman* would certainly go a long way if we were to instill in our children in America the art of endurance and tolerance for the sake of harmony.

As it is now, most of us spend a lot of time and energy stewing over and fighting things that really "can't be helped."

Child Rearing in Japan

I observed something very interesting when I first arrived in Japan that puzzled me greatly. One night, when I was walking home to my apartment, I passed a neighbor's house where there was a child crying and pounding frantically on the door.

I paused to see what was going on and to see if there was anything I could do to help. At this point in the incident I noticed his mother peering out of the window at him. The boy, who was 8 or 9 years old, was yelling *Okaasan...iretekudasai*! ("Mother, let me in!").

She ignored his pleas for a few more moments, and then finally opened the door to let him in. What just happened? This whole scene that transpired before my eyes left me bewildered, confused and even worried about the child rearing habits of this mother.

That same evening a Japanese friend came to visit me and I recounted the entire episode to him. His first response was one of admiration: "She is a good mother because she is teaching him to be a better person...."

Well, needless to say, I was further confused at his reasoning behind leaving a child outside as punishment. My friend then asked me how Americans punish children for misbehaving. I explained to him that there is a variety of methods, some very mild and some more severe.

Sometimes we correct children's behavior with a firm spanking to withholding allowance money or sending them to their room. On this last point my friend said, "So, basically the same way, right?" "No! We don't lock children outside of the house!" I countered. He said, "No, you lock them inside, by sending them to their room."

Hmmm, he had a very valid point. There really isn't much difference in the "method," only in the "means." The end result of both approaches is to discipline the child for bad behavior, and to teach the child not to repeat the behavior in the future. After all, the important thing is that the child learns right from wrong in order to be a productive member of society.

This difference in child-rearing and parental discipline fascinated me—it was the opposite way of doing it, yet at the same time it was very similar. The methods could be regarded as equally logical, but different. The way of viewing the punishment was based on cultural considerations, but the intended outcome of the punishment was virtually the same.

For instance, an American child would love to be sent outside of the house for punishment—the child would run and play freely, reveling in his/her independence and freedom. A Japanese child on the other hand would prefer to be inside where s/he is afforded the security and warmth of the group (in this case the family).

Perhaps the American child finds the forced solitude of his/her room unbearable. Both punishments exclude the child from where they would prefer to be, whether it is inside…or outside.

In general, it seems to me that in America we tend to be stricter with children from an earlier age. Japanese children have a lot more flexibility as to what is considered inappropriate behavior by their parents than their American counterparts do.

In Japan, a small child who misbehaves in public is largely ignored by bystanders; an American child who acts in the same manner would probably receive a stern talking to and a light smack on the behind (if really bad), right in front of the bystanders.

Once when I had some Japanese people over with their children, I was shocked to walk into my living room and see three of the toddlers jumping on my sofa and chairs. The mothers were sitting nearby chatting, seemingly unaware of what their children were doing. I quickly suggested we all go outside on the patio.

Admittedly, my house is not "kid friendly"; another friend who has a very well-behaved child visited recently and her son said, "This house is really breakable." There are just too many tempting artifacts from my trips to touch and handle for little ones who are naturally curious and inquisitive.

Although Japan and the United States have different methods and means for disciplining children, parents from both countries strive for the same results—healthy, well-adjusted children who are learning from experience how to behave properly and appropriately in society.

Unique Festivals

Japanese people celebrate just about every aspect of daily family life in some sort of festival or celebration. Many of these customs are quite old and enveloped with tradition, sometimes based on superstition, but mostly formed out of religious beliefs.

There is one very interesting Buddhist tradition, *Hari-kuyou*, which occurs on February 8th every year. This ceremony commemorates a type of "sayonara send-off" for broken sewing needles. It is believed that these tiny instruments that gave of themselves freely to sew and mend the clothes that are worn on a daily basis need to be eulogized in a fitting and reverent ceremony. After all, without these very useful items, clothing could not be made; torn apparel could not be repaired.

Girls' schools, and specifically sewing or design schools, celebrate this festival every year. An elaborate altar is prepared with three levels; food offerings of fruits and cakes are often placed on the top level; on the second level is placed a huge cake of tofu; and on the third level, sewing related accessories like scissors, thread and thimbles are delicately arranged.

The broken needles are then gingerly pushed into the soft tofu by the persons who used these utensils, offering them a comfortable and respectful final resting place. Each needle is believed to have a soul, having given of itself a unique and useful service to its owner. If the needle is revered properly and kept in a secure place until the ceremony, then it can't be lost to inflict injury upon some unsuspecting soul who might step on it or inadvertently prick a finger with it.

A dear Japanese friend of mine in Hirosaki used to be a principal of a girl's home economics school that had an advanced fashion design course. Every year, she and her students would perform this ceremony. They always invited outside dressmakers and seamstresses to attend and partake in this very unique tradition.

I had the great fortune to observe this fascinating custom many years ago. I was impressed with the reverence that the women possessed in placing the no longer usable needles into the cake of tofu. It is a charming custom, indeed.

Another equally charming custom, that is much more spectacular to the eye, is the annual Girl's Day celebration that takes place on March 3rd. Every year, little girls all over Japan celebrate this very unique and special festival by dressing up in *kimono* and inviting their friends, cousins and family to come and view their doll collections.

The festival is called *Hina Matsuri* (Doll Festival) which also marks "Girl's Day," the day when Japanese celebrate all things girlish. These dolls are not your ordinary, run-of-the-mill play-things that are played with in the sandbox and in the bathtub. These are hand-made, elaborately dressed and adorned dolls that become keepsakes and family heirlooms.

When I first came to Japan, a teacher invited me to his home for dinner and to view his daughter's doll collection. Initially I wasn't so keen on going because I imagined the dolls would be a hodge-podge of items the daughter had collected and played with from the time she was a toddler.

After dinner, the little girl brought us to a special *tatami* (straw mat) room and when she opened the sliding door, there before us was a display of the like I had never witnessed before in my life. I stood there in awe at the spectacular arrangement of the most exquisitely crafted dolls I had ever seen.

The whole display covered an entire wall. They were all meticulously arranged on a graduated display frame that had at least eight, possibly more, levels. The entire frame was hidden by a rich, red felt covering. At the top were the dolls that represented the emperor and empress; each level below contained dolls from the imperial court. Around each doll contained various miniature objects like cabinets, folding screens, carriages, and suits of armor with swords.

This girl's mother explained to me that the bulk of the dolls were hers and her mother's. When she married, she brought it with her and has now passed it on to her daughter, adding keepsake items throughout the years. This woman's daughter will eventually pass it on to her future daughter. New doll sets can cost thousands of dollars.

These dolls are never played with, but only displayed during the *hina matsuri* period, for about two weeks. I suppose this custom most resembles an American Christmas tree and its ornaments in that it is carefully displayed, not touched or handled in anyway, and special ornaments are saved and then passed on to succeeding generations.

Any little girl would feel special during this festival; after all it is her day to celebrate being a little girl.

The Sneeze

A custom that I am used to in America, but one that is not practiced here in Japan (and one that I admittedly miss to a certain degree) is saying "bless you!" after someone sneezes.

One of my first culture shocks after arriving in Japan happened when I sneezed out loud in my office. No one said a word. Everyone went about their business and ignored my sneeze completely.

This surprised me because I had never really stopped to think of the custom of saying "bless you" as being Western and not Eastern. The first few times I sneezed in front of people in Japan, I made a point to say "excuse me" or "pardon me" in Japanese.

This reaction on my part confused them, because they had no idea what I was referring to when I asked to be excused and pardoned. I guess I felt self-conscious and even a little embarrassed for sneezing. Back home, people almost always acknowledge your sneeze and I missed having someone say "bless you" or the equivalent in Japanese (which there isn't one).

Finally, I asked my supervisor why in Japan no one says anything after one sneezes. He explained that it isn't customary to bring attention to someone who has just sneezed, but instead it is more polite to just ignore it. I found this small cultural difference fascinating.

In America, acknowledging a sneeze is such an embedded custom that everyone, everywhere replies to someone's sneeze. This training begins in childhood. It is so common that strangers on the street will bless you if you sneeze.

Why do we say "bless you" after someone sneezes? This custom has superstitious as well as religious origins based on Judeo-Christian tradition. This custom has a very interesting history behind it, stemming from Western religion and not Eastern religion (which explains why the Japanese don't have this custom or an equivalent one).

It was believed by early Christians and Jews that when a person sneezed, his/her body became vulnerable and susceptible to outside, evil forces—the devil could enter the body at the moment of the sneeze and take control of it. To prevent this, someone standing close must say "God bless you!" to keep the demon out. Hence the tradition began.

I taught my colleagues in my office this custom of saying "bless you." After that, whenever anyone sneezed, a raucous chorus of "bless you" rang through the office followed by a wild roar of laughter. It was fun for them to participate in a Western custom that is not practiced in Japan.

One custom in America that I don't miss here in Japan is the habit of blowing your nose in a cloth handkerchief after you sneeze, and carrying it all day, stuffed in your pocket. This custom surprises many Japanese who visit the United States; Japanese all use handkerchiefs, but only to wipe their faces and to dry their hands.

Most public bathrooms don't have toilet tissue or hand towels. Most Japanese people, as a matter of course, carry small packets of tissue (many businesses, as modes of advertisement, pass these out freely at train stations and in front of big department stores). Since public toilets don't have hand towels, most people carry a handkerchief to dry their hands after washing them. In the summer, small towels and handkerchiefs are carried to wipe the sweat off their faces. Japanese summers are notoriously hot and humid.

I can imagine what Japanese people would think after seeing Americans blow their noses in handkerchiefs then promptly proceeding to stuff the soiled cloths into their pockets: Are they going to wipe their faces or dry their hands with those dirty handkerchiefs?

In Japan, there is a social stigma about blowing your nose in public. It is considered rude and impolite. If unavoidable, Japanese people try to be very discreet and unobtrusive when doing so. Of course, Americans are not bothered by people blowing their noses in public…but probably would be if the same people then used the soiled handkerchiefs to wipe their faces and hands.

Graduation

Since the Japanese school year begins in April, the end of the school year is in February. Graduation (from elementary, junior and senior high, and college and university) takes place in mid-March.

University graduation is always a happy time...but it is also a sad time. It's joyous because the students with whom you spent the last four years have reached their goal and are graduating, going onto pursue their dreams; it is melancholy because you have to say goodbye to some really great students to whom you have become attached.

Teachers who say they don't have "favorites" are liars. Of course, the party line is that all students are equal and everyone is liked the same, blah, blah, blah. In theory this should be true, but in reality, it is only natural to be drawn to students with whom you feel you have made a marked difference in their educational career or have connected with on a personal level.

It isn't always the "smarties" that become the favorites. For me, the students who really grow from the educational experience, personally and intellectually, and who work hard to be the best they can be are the ones that hold a special place in my heart. Undoubtedly, these are the students who will keep me posted of their achievements and drop by my office to see me for years to come. Nothing thrills me more than to see former students succeed in their professional and personal lives.

Graduation in Japan doesn't have the same type of pomp and circumstance that graduation does in the United States. There is great formality, but students don't don cap and gowns and parents don't cheer raucously from the sidelines when their son or daughter's name is called. It is a very serious affair, indeed. The song of choice at graduation in Japan is "Auld Lang Syne."

At my university, the majority of the women wear an apron-like garment called a *hakuma*. This is worn over their actual *kimono*, usually the one they received when they turned twenty years of age. A woman's *hakuma* has a high-waist and usually is solid in color, bright or subdued, depending upon the taste of the wearer. The men almost always wear dark suits.

The morning of graduation is a busy time for hair-dressers around the city where I live. The place where I get my haircut begins coiffing the women's hair in elaborate and intricate designs at 5:00 am; they are booked solid until about a half hour before the graduation ceremony begins.

When I first started teaching, the graduates were all very prim and proper with their traditional wear and clothing—shoes, handbags, and hair ornaments were all very traditional. Today, even women who wear the traditional *hakuma* may forego wearing traditional Japanese footwear, and opt for platform shoes or boots.

Instead of having their straight, jet black hair arranged in a traditional bun like before, many students today have perms and color their hair; they add more modern ornaments that are "hip" today, as well as having brightly colored hair-extensions added to their natural hair to be "in-style."

After graduation is over, many students go directly to a professional photographer to have a graduation portrait taken in their formal clothes. It seems that most university campuses have a professional photographer located nearby. This once a year activity probably draws enough business to make it worthwhile to be located near a college campus.

A nice custom in Japan is that many of the graduating seniors' *kohai* (underclassman or juniors) wait outside to present their *sempai* (upperclassman or seniors) with bouquets of flowers and small gifts. Of course, tons of photos are taken with teachers, friends and family members.

Every year, a number of parents come to me to thank me personally for teaching their son or daughter. This always pleases me greatly to know that the parents appreciate the hard work of the teachers who educate their children.

Shortly, after graduation, we teachers must attend the opening ceremony for the incoming freshman students. One cycle ends and another begins.

Coffee Shops

Drinking coffee in Japan has become an art form. Perhaps, in part, this is due to the ritualized manner in which Japanese traditionally have prepared and drank green tea. The "tea ceremony" is very solemn and methodical; people apprentice for years to become a tea master.

Coffee, on the other hand, is an imported item that doesn't have the same historical restrictions and tradition that green tea has, but has become a part of Japanese ritual all the same. Coffee, as a preferred drink, has really taken off in recent years and is a daily part of a Japanese adult person's life.

After World War II, coffee and coffee shops (*kissaten*) gained in popularity. Slowly, but steadily, coffee shops became a normal part of a city's business landscape. Today, coffee shops can be found in literally every town and village in Japan. Canned coffee is available in vending machines, as well as in every supermarket in the country.

These coffee shops, though, are not the average coffee shop image we have in America, with the bottomless-cup-of-coffee, shiny counters, with donuts or wedges of pies on racks behind the counter. Instead, these places offer a person a diversion to their daily routine; a place to escape from the rigors of their life or workplace.

Kissaten offer elegance and a reprieve from the hustle-bustle of the big cities to escape and relax in, over a piping hot, hand-brewed cup of coffee. Usually these coffee shops have very few seats, are quiet, and have a particular ambience according to the specific tastes of the owner.

There is a *kissaten* in the prefectural seat that I love to go to that has an Austrian theme. Once you walk through the door, it is as if you were transported to a coffee shop in Vienna. All of the décor and furnishings are painstakingly done to replicate a Viennese cake shop.

The owner had lived in Vienna, fell in love with it, and brought back with him to Japan a dream to open an authentic Austrian coffee shop. He succeeded, and now has a thriving business catering to housewives who meet there with their friends to enjoy afternoon tea. He is very clever in that he offers live classical piano music in the afternoons and has expanded to include a delicious variety of German and Austrian cakes. I could spend hours in there.

Other coffee shops might feature classical or jazz music, a Latin American or French renaissance décor—the list is endless. Somewhere in Japan, there is most likely a coffee shop with every type of theme and décor imaginable. The number of coffee shops in Japan must be in the tens of thousands.

American-style coffee shops like Mr. Donuts do exist in Japan. A cup of coffee out of a brewed pot is about $2–3 for a bottomless cup. These are mainly frequented by junior and senior high school students, business people in a rush, or regular folk who are either in a hurry and want a quick cup of coffee, or who feel uncomfortable in the swankier *kissaten*.

The real, personalized cup of coffee can only be found in the true *kissaten* where the owner, who also serves as preparer and waiter, stands behind the counter serving and chatting easily with the customers who regularly frequent the shop. One or two small tables may also be available for people who want to sit and read, or those who come in small groups to talk quietly amongst themselves.

A cup of coffee that is purchased in a *kissaten* can cost between $5–10 per cup (depending upon how upscale and trendy the shop is). It seems pricey, but I've been told that although the coffee is delicious, that really isn't what you're paying for—you are actually purchasing the right to the space. Buying one cup of coffee entitles you to stay as long as you want, reading, writing, chatting or simply relaxing.

One reason why people in Japan love going to coffee shops to meet with friends and colleagues is that they don't have to worry about having people come to their homes (especially if the home is small and cramped). Also, many times it is just easier to meet outside in a central location than to try to maneuver all of the winding streets trying to find a particular person's home. For whatever reasons, coffee shops in Japan are here to stay.

Japanese-Style English

A first time visitor to Japan is often surprised at how much English is used on signs and in daily conversations; the problem is that many times it is either incorrect or misspelled.

Don't get me wrong, I am all for the Japanese adopting English as a Second Language (that is a large part of my work here in Japan), and I think it is perfectly natural for the Japanese language to adapt and use English for its own purposes (after all the English language is filled with borrowed terms, phrases and words from a variety of other languages—for example, "sheriff "was originally an Arabic word). But I do find it humorous sometimes when I come across a truly outrageous sign or t-shirt. It makes me laugh out loud.

The Japanese are gradually creating a new language that can best be described as "Japlish"—part Japanese and part English. Usually these are words or phrases that have a very specific Japanese meaning, but use English words in such a way that a native speaker may be able to guess what the intended meaning is, but often times cannot.

The downside to this is that when I return home I sometimes use this new language and people have no idea what I am talking about. I get so used to hearing it here, that it sounds natural…even normal to my native ears.

For instance, once when I visited friends back home I suggested that we go to a "live house." They looked at me like deer in headlights. I said, "You know, a 'live house'…wouldn't that be fun? Finally, my friend said, "Well, it would be fun if I knew what the heck you were talking about!?"

I then realized that I had inadvertently used a Japanese term meaning "an establishment where one can enjoy live music." So, to me it made perfect sense, because it is clearly understood using Japanese linguistic logic to refer to these types of places as "live houses."

Some other examples include "silver seat," "terminal hotel," "skinship", and "one room mansion." The first of these refers to seats that are reserved for elderly people, hence the term "silver" because many senior citizens have silver-colored hair.

A "terminal hotel" is a place of lodging that is either connected to or very near a major train station. The affection that is displayed via touching between good friends (not lovers), siblings and or parents and children is called "skinship"—a hybrid between skin and friendship.

An efficiency apartment in Japan is called a "one room mansion" which is really a misnomer because these are usually very small, cramped and nothing like a "mansion" in the true sense of the word.

Many everyday items use an English-like word that have been adopted into the Japanese language by giving it a "katakana" pronunciation: *terebi* (television), *sutereo* (stereo), *doa* (door), *teeburu* (table), *beto* (bed), *kohikappu* (coffee cup), and *sofaa* (sofa) to name a few.

In addition, many English terms that are adapted to Japanese get shortened. A very popular term used by the media here is *sekuhara* which is a contraction of "sexual harassment." Others include *bodicon* for "body conscious" which refers to people (usually women) who worry about their appearance and body shape; *hean-uudo* for "hair nude" or a photograph that has visible pubic hair; and *eakon* for air conditioner.

The list is endless and is continuing to grow everyday. It is so difficult for elderly people to keep up with all of the new phrases and terms that it's no wonder they can't understand a significant amount of popular television anymore; most young people and *tarento* (for "talent" meaning entertainers) regularly use this new form of Japanese riddled with English phrases and words.

It's not only English. The Japanese have borrowed from many other languages, including Portuguese, Spanish, Dutch, French and German. Once when I had to get an x-ray I had a difficult time finding the proper room because I assumed it would be written with an English derivation. The word in Japanese was written *rento gen* which is taken from the German language. Since I have no German language ability at all, I finally had to ask by describing where it was I needed to go. Usually, an English speaker can get by rather easily using Japanized English, but not always.

Getting Older

Recently, I had a life changing experience. While flying back to my prefecture from Tokyo, high above Honshu Island, a flight attendant innocently referred to me as *ojisan* or "uncle" to her colleague.

Face to face, service people refer to customers as *okyakusama* ("customer" with a title of respect), but she was telling her workmate to get me a drink which she didn't have on her cart. Her colleague asked "who?" and she motioned toward me and basically said "that middle-aged uncle over there." Of course, I wasn't supposed to hear it, but I did. This innocent remark certainly changed the way I view myself from that day forward.

In Japan, there is no real equivalent to ma'am, sir, Mr., Mrs., or Miss. Of course, if the person knows your name, they will say the family name followed by *san* or *sama*—both titles of respect.

Even students tend to use the family name when speaking to and about friends their own age. First names are normally reserved for family members and really close, childhood friends. All company employees tend to refer to each other more formally than their counterparts in the United States do, using the family name and the title "san."

Anyway, this had never happened to me before! I am at that critical age where people can regard me as an *oniisan* (older brother) or *ojisan* (middle-aged uncle) which I tend to think of as being much older than how old I think I am.

I guess I am at that in-between age where I theoretically could still be regarded as an *oniisan* by much older people, but I appear to be an *ojisan* to the much younger twenty-somethings. Actually, at 40-plus years of age, I do fall into the latter category officially…but I still don't feel it.

Aren't I still boyish with my early Beetles' haircut? Maybe it's my mustache. Perhaps I should get rid of it to shave off a couple of years to give me some breathing room for the approaching inevitability that I will be routinely addressed as *ojisan*.

Once at a barbecue, a friend's child who is half-American, half-Japanese called me *baba* which means "granny." His father said that all foreigners to him are "granny." This didn't make me feel any better. Granted, he was only 2-years-old, but I hope his grandmother's mustache wasn't as thick as mine. I'll risk it and keep the mustache—being called "uncle" is much more preferred than "granny" at my tender age.

It is difficult for me to know how to address people in Japan for the same reason. If you say *obasan* (auntie) to a woman who does not yet consider herself to be matronly, it can be quite offensive. *Okusan* is a term given to married women, but in today's world, not every woman of marriageable age is necessarily married.

English is so much easier because the terms "ma'am" and "sir" cover the whole gamut. The first time I was called "sir" in the States was a few years back when I bought gasoline. The attendant called out to me, "Sir!" I just kept on walking, not thinking he was addressing me. I think of my father as being "sir," not me.

Age is a funny thing. When we are young, we can't wait to be older, and once we are older, we want time to stop. You can't open a magazine in Japan or in America without being bombarded with rejuvenation remedies to look young again and gimmicks to help you achieve that youthful glow.

It doesn't help either that every model, actor and entertainer is seemingly at the prime of their youth. They gyrate about, strutting their youthfulness for all to see. Good for them; they should enjoy it while it lasts, because it won't last forever. I'm living proof of that.

As I get older, the things that bother me the most are the simple tasks I enjoyed doing just a few years ago with much more ease and vigor than I do today. For instance, running up and down the stairs was as effortless as breathing. Once I turned forty it seems that a switch went off inside me that caused my knees to snap, crackle and pop when descending the stairs first thing in the morning.

Don't misunderstand me. I consider myself quite fit and am very healthy according to my last check-up. It just seems that I have lost the edge I once had—my pace is slower, my body is bigger, and the hair on my head is less full and thick.

Actually, for all of my ranting and raving, I don't really mind getting older. All the promises of youthfulness in the world wouldn't convince me to trade my life experience and wisdom gained from making mistakes for a younger model…or worse yet, to start over.

I'm middle-aged…there, I said it. As much as I hate to admit it, I am warming up to the idea of being an *ojisan*. There are some perks, like more respect, and seats being offered to you on trains and buses. I guess I actually embrace the aging process and I look forward to the time when I am referred to as *ojiisan* (grandpa).

About the Author

Todd Jay Leonard lives, writes, and teaches in Japan where he is a university professor. He has published extensively in academic journals, magazines and newspapers on cross-cultural and TEFL themes. His publications include *Crossing Cultures: America and Japan* (Kenkyusha, 1992); *Extra! Extra! Read All About It!* (Kinseido, 1994); *Team-Teaching Together: A Bilingual Resource Handbook for JTEs and AETs* (Taishukan, 1994); *Talk, Talk: American-Style* (Macmillan Languagehouse, 1996); *Words to Write By: Developing Writing Skills through Quotations* (Macmillan Languagehouse, 1997); *The Better Half: Exploring the Changing Roles of Men and Women with Current Newspaper Articles* (Macmillan Languagehouse, 1997); *East Meets West: An American in Japan* (Kenkyusha, 1998); *East Meets West: Problems and Solutions—Understanding Misunderstandings between JTEs and ALTs* (Taishukan, 1999); *Trendy Traditions: A Cross Cultural Skills-Based Reader of Essays on the United States* (Macmillan Languagehouse, 2002); and *Business as Usual: An Integrated Approach to Learning English* (Seibido, 2003).

0-595-28309-8